Pro-Mgmt.

The Restaurant: From Concept to Operation

FOURTH EDITION

Student Workbook

National Restaurant Association
EDUCATIONAL FOUNDATION

JOHN WILEY & SONS, INC.

Published by John Wiley & Sons, Inc., Hoboken, New Jersey

Published simultaneously in Canada.

This publication is designed to provide accurate and authoritative information in regard to the subject matter covered. It is sold with the understanding that the publisher is not engaged in rendering professional services. If professional advice or other expert assistance is required, the services of a competent professional should be sought.

Library of Congress Cataloging-in-Publication Data:

ISBN: 0-471-70867-4

Printed in the United States of America

10 9 8 7 6 5 4 3 2 1

CONTENTS

INTRODUCTION

The Restaurant: From Concept to Operation, Fourth Edition, will introduce a broad variety of restaurant functions. As future foodservice managers, you will find the overview useful both in planning future study and directing you toward satisfactory career choices.

The course begins with an overview of restaurant operations and then looks at menus, cost control, and financial matters. Legal issues, the restaurant staff, employee training, and equipping the kitchen are covered next. The course then discusses the fundamentals of marketing and purchasing and concludes with a section on customer service, laws and regulations, and sanitation.

The ProMgmt.® Program

How to Earn a ProMgmt. Certificate of Course Completion

To earn a ProMgmt. Certificate of Course Completion, a student must complete all student workbook exercises and receive a passing score on the final examination.

Each student who submits an examination answer sheet to the NRAEF will receive a student number. Please make a record of it; this number will identify you during your present and future coursework with the NRAEF.

ProMgmt. certificate requirements are administered exclusively through colleges and other educational institutions that offer ProMgmt. courses and examinations.

If you are not currently enrolled in a ProMgmt. course and would like to earn a ProMgmt. certificate, please contact your local educational institution to see if they are willing to administer the ProMgmt. certificate requirements for non-enrolled students. You can also visit www.nraef.org for a list of ProMgmt. Partner schools. ProMgmt. Partner schools offer seven or more courses that include administration of the ProMgmt. certificate requirements.

The NRAEF leaves it to the discretion of each educational institution offering ProMgmt. courses to decide whether or not that institution will administer the ProMgmt. certificate requirements to non-enrolled students. If an institution does administer ProMgmt. certificate requirements to non-enrolled students, that institution may charge an additional fee, of an amount determined by that institution, for the administration of the ProMgmt. certificate requirements.

Course Materials

This course consists of the text, *The Restaurant, Fourth Edition,* by John R. Walker and Donald E. Lundberg, the student workbook, and a final examination. The examination is the final section of your course and is sent to an instructor for administration, then returned to the NRAEF for grading.

Each chapter consists of:

- Learning Objectives
- Chapter Study Outline
- Chapter Check-in
- Answers to Chapter Check-in (at the end of the workbook)

At the end of the workbook you will find:

- An 80-question practice test
- Answers to the practice test

The objectives indicate what you can expect to learn from the course, and are designed to help you organize your studying and concentrate on important topics and explanations. Refer to the objectives frequently to make sure you are meeting them.

The exercises help you check how well you've learned the concepts in each chapter. These will be graded by your instructor.

An 80-question Practice Test appears at the end of the workbook. All the questions are multiple-choice and have four possible answers. Circle the best answer to each question, as in this example:

Who was the first president of the United States?
A. Thomas Jefferson
B. *George Washington*
C. Benjamin Franklin
D. John Adams

Answers to the Practice Test follow in the workbook so that you can grade your own work.

The Final Exam

All examinations can first be graded by your instructor and then officially graded again by the NRAEF. If you do not receive a passing grade on the examination, you may request a retest. A retest fee will be charged for the second examination.

Study Tips

Since you have already demonstrated an interest in furthering your foodservice education by registering for this NRAEF course, you know that your next step is study preparation. We have included some specific study aids that you might find useful.

- Build studying time into your routine. If you hold a full-time job, you need to take a realistic approach to studying. Set aside a specific time and place to study, and stick to your routine as closely as possible. Your study area should have room for your course materials and any other necessary study aids. If possible, your area should be away from family traffic.
- Discuss with family members your study goals and your need for a quiet place and private time to work. They might want to help you draw up a study schedule that will be satisfactory to everyone.
- Keep a study log. You can record what chapter you completed, a list of topics studied, the time you spent, and how well you scored on the Chapter Check-ins and Practice Test.
- Work at your own pace, but move ahead steadily. The following tips should help you get the most value from your lessons.
    1. Look over the objectives carefully. They list what you are expected to know for the examination.
    2. Read the chapters carefully, and don't hesitate to mark your text—it will help you later. Mark passages that seem especially important and those that seem difficult, as you might want to reread them later.
    3. Try to read an entire chapter at a time. Even though more than one chapter might be assigned at time, you might find you can carefully read only one chapter in a sitting.
    4. When you have finished reading the chapter, go back and check the highlights and any notes you have made. These will help you review for the examination.

Reviewing for the Final Exam

Once you have completed the final exercise and Practice Test, you will have several items to use for your examination review. If you have highlighted important points in the textbook, you can review them. If you have made notes in the margins, check them to be sure you have answered any questions that arose when you read the material. Reread certain sections if necessary. Finally, you should go over your exercises.

The ProMgmt.® Program

The National Restaurant Association Educational Foundation's ProMgmt. program is designed to provide foodservice students and professionals with a solid foundation of practical knowledge and information. Each course focuses on a specific management area. Students who earn ProMgmt. certificates improve their chances of:
- Earning NRAEF Undergraduate Scholarships.
- Gaining management jobs within the foodservice and restaurant industry.

For more information on both the ProMgmt. program and scholarships, please contact the NRAEF at 800.765.2122 (312.715.1010 in Chicagoland), or visit our Web site at **www.nraef.org**.

CHAPTER 1

INTRODUCTION

Learning Objectives

After reading this chapter, you should be able to:

1.1   Discus reasons why some people open restaurants.

1.2   List some liabilities of restaurant operation.

1.3   Outline the history of restaurants.

1.4   Compare the advantages and disadvantages of buying, building, and franchising restaurants.

Chapter 1 Study Outline

1. People open restaurants because it is interesting and challenging, and it has the potential to make investors wealthy.
2. Successful restaurateurs need considerable experience, planning, financial support, and energy.
3. Restaurant owners cite steady hard work and the ability to work well with people as the two major keys to their success.
4. Excessive fatigue from long hours working in a restaurant can jeopardize a person's emotional and physical well being.
5. There is typically little job security for managers working for others, since a change in ownership often means management will be replaced.
6. The term "restaurant" is derived from the restoratives served by M. Boulanger at his all-night tavern in eighteenth-century Paris.
7. In 1794, Jean-Baptist Gilbert Paypalt opened the first foodservice establishment called a restaurant in Boston. However, because of its style, New York City's Delmonico's, which opened in 1827, is often credited as the first American restaurant.
8. While restaurant-failure rates may be exaggerated, the financial risk of opening a restaurant is high. Many foodservice startups have successful concepts but lack the funds to stay open long enough to establish the business.

9. Family-owned restaurants often succeed because family members can work for lower salaries, with a reduced risk of theft. However, stress from long hours at work and differences of opinion often cause families to splinter.

10. Studies show that restaurants that remain open for at least three years have the best chance for survival.

11. Before deciding whether to buy, build, franchise, or manage someone else's restaurant, it is necessary to consider a host of factors, including economic conditions, potential market, competition, and capital available from investors.

12. Buying an existing restaurant can reduce risk, if the weaknesses of the existing business can be overcome. However, it may be exceedingly difficult to overcome a poor reputation acquired by the previous owner.

13. Building a new restaurant requires the largest financial investment. At the same time, it offers the greatest potential for self-expression and personal fulfillment.

14. Franchising has the least risk, since the concept has already been tested, but it offers owners little flexibility.

15. Managing a restaurant for an owner involves the least financial risk, but can still be emotionally draining if the restaurant fails.

Chapter 1 Exercises

1. Indicate whether the following statements are true (T) or false (F).

_____ a. Most restaurants are neither big winners nor big losers.

_____ b. Opening a franchise offers the greatest opportunity for restaurant owners to express themselves.

_____ c. The term restaurant comes from the soups sold by M. Boulanger in Paris.

_____ d. Paypalt opened the first French restaurant in the U.S. when he immigrated to Boston.

_____ e. Many restaurant startups fail because they are undercapitalized.

_____ f. Family-owned restaurants often succeed because family members never steal.

_____ g. The failure rate for new restaurants falls after three years.

_____ h. Buying an existing restaurant offers the least financial risk because the mistakes of the previous owner can be overcome.

_____ i. Franchises have a better chance for success because most of the concept's issues have been addressed.

_____ j. The goal of most franchisers is to keep fees low.

L.O. 1.2, 1.3, 1.4

2. List five reasons why people invest in restaurants.

- _____
- _____
- _____
- _____
- _____

L.O. 1.1

Chapter 1 Check-in

1. In the restaurant business, there is no substitute for

    A. intelligence.
    B. experience.
    C. luck.
    D. social skills.

    L.O. 1.1

2. Most successful restaurant owners believe they beat the odds by

    A. spending working capital on strong advertising campaigns.
    B. devoting extra time to their family and friends.
    C. going to college.
    D. working hard and persevering.

    L.O. 1.1

3. The best way to understand the difficulties involved in restaurant ownership is to

    A. enroll in a culinary academy.
    B. take classes at a junior college.
    C. work in a restaurant.
    D. eat out often.

    L.O. 1.2

4. Restaurant employees often work long hours and are susceptible to

    A. poor financial decisions.
    B. weight gain.
    C. mononucleosis.
    D. repetitive motion injuries.

    L.O. 1.2

5. The bulk of food sales at restaurants occur

    A. on Mondays.
    B. during weekends.
    C. at holidays.
    D. during major sporting events.

    L.O. 1.2

6. The original *restorantes* served by M. Boulanger in Paris were

    A. hot drinks made with rum.
    B. sugary desserts topped with chocolate sauce.
    C. special soups.
    D. casseroles made with sheep's feet.

    L.O. 1.3

7. Often credited as the first American restaurant in the U.S., Delmonico's was opened in which city?

    A. New York
    B. Chicago
    C. New Orleans
    D. Boston

L.O. 1.3

8. Recent studies show that restaurants do not close as often for financial reasons as they do for

    A. personal problems.
    B. health-department violations.
    C. high employee turnover.
    D. fire damage.

L.O. 1.4

9. The type of restaurant that is the least expensive to start and operate is a

    A. franchise.
    B. sandwich shop.
    C. steak house.
    D. fine-dining establishment.

L.O. 1.4

10. Buying a franchise

    A. eliminates the risk of failure.
    B. reduces the risk of failure.
    C. ensures the restaurant will do well in its location.
    D. has no effect on the risk of failure.

L.O. 1.4

CHAPTER 2

KINDS AND CHARACTERISTICS OF RESTAURANTS AND THEIR OWNERS

Learning Objectives

After reading this chapter, you should be able to:

2.1   List and describe the various kinds of restaurants.

2.2   Compare and contrast chain and independent restaurant operations.

2.3   Briefly describe the lives and contributions of prominent, past, and present

restaurateurs.

Chapter 2 Study Outline

1. Restaurants are broadly classified as quick-serve, family, casual, dinner house, and fine dining.

2. The types of restaurants are constantly changing, and today's market leaders may not even exist in the future.

3. The most successful leaders in the restaurant industry usually are hardworking, willing to learn from their mistakes, and take full advantage of their natural public-relations skills.

4. Quick-serve restaurants aim to serve the maximum number of patrons in the least amount of time.

5. Regional burger chains can compete successfully against the multimillion-dollar advertising campaigns of the big, multinational chains.

6. Mexican-style food is relatively inexpensive because of the small percentage of meat used, reducing food costs.

7. Despite higher-than-average food costs, steakhouse owners often choose to open this type of restaurant because it offers a limited menu and caters to an easily defined market.

8. Customers in fine-dining establishments expect all food, drink, and service to be of the highest quality and are willing to pay extra for it. The entire dining experience must stimulate the visitor's visual, auditory, and psychological senses.

9. Historically, ethnic restaurants were small and family owned, but over the past ten years some have grown to become national chains.

10. Theme restaurants are built around an idea focused on fun and fantasy. They have a short life cycle and often earn a large portion of their profits from merchandise sales.

11. Chef-owned operations benefit from having a highly experienced and very motivated person in charge, but often suffer because the chefs do not have enough business knowledge to manage the financial side.

12. A number of women have succeeded in the restaurant business. According to the National Restaurant Association, women held sixty-eight percent of all supervisory positions in 1997.

13. Bakery/cafés serve coffee as well as fresh baked goods. Today, many of them manufacture their baked goods at central commissaries, and then finish the baking process on site.

14. The Internet is expanding home delivery from pizza and ethnic food to include dinners from upscale restaurants available for homes and hotel rooms.

Chapter 2 Exercises

1. Identify the restaurant type described by the following statements. Some answers may be used more than once.

   a. Food costs are relatively low because a smaller percentage of meat is used.

   _____

   b. These have limited menus and a well-identified market.

   _____

   c. The goal is to serve the maximum number of customers in the least amount of time.

   _____

   d. These resemble railroad dining cars

   _____

   e. Larger ones use a central commissary system to prep products and finish cooking them at their final destination.

   _____

   f. Limited seating is available, with an average check running higher than sixty dollars.

   _____

   g. Improvements in aquaculture are reducing the cost of operating them.

   _____

   h. This growing segment takes orders over the phone or the Internet before sending out the meal.

   _____

   i. Cooking relies heavily on the use of a wok.

   _____

j. Much of the profits come from the sale of merchandise.

_____

k. This type of restaurant is located in a limited geographical area.

_____

l. While they have a highly motivated person in charge, this type of restaurant usually needs a partner with extensive business sense.

_____

m. It is the most common type of ethnic restaurant in the U.S.

_____

n. Guests expect tableware and architectural features that are highly refined.

_____

o. These restaurants got their start from immigrants preparing familiar food in large portions at a low price.

_____

L.O. 2.1

2. List three characteristics shared by the restaurateurs profiled in Chapter 2.

- _____

- _____

- _____

L.O. 2.3

Chapter 2 Check-in

1. The most popular eateries in the U.S. are

   A. family-dining operations.
   B. hamburger chains.
   C. fried-chicken chains.
   D. steakhouses.

   L.O. 2.1

2. Fine-dining restaurants invest heavily in

   A. humorous television commercials.
   B. computer systems to increase table turnover.
   C. public-relations campaigns.
   D. drive-thru windows.

   L.O. 2.1

3. If its menu offers spinach pasta noodles, the restaurant is probably

    A. Indian.
    B. French.
    C. Chinese.
    D. Northern Italian.

   L.O. 2.1

4. Szechwan cooking is best known for its use of

    A. hot peppers.
    B. marinated steaks.
    C. heavy sauces.
    D. bite-sized dumplings.

   L.O. 2.1

5. This type of restaurant often has very high food costs but exceptionally low labor costs.

    A. Fine-dining establishment
    B. Steakhouse
    C. Sandwich shop
    D. Bakery/Café

   L.O. 2.1

6. The Colonel began promoting his secret blend of herbs and spices when he was

    A. 33.
    B. 44.
    C. 55.
    D. 66.

   L.O. 2.3

7. Chef-owned operations often fail because

    A. the chefs believe their names alone will draw customers.
    B. the chefs do not usually have the business skills to run the restaurant.
    C. a marital dispute can lead to a divorce and a split of the assets.
    D. All of the above

   L.O. 2.1

8. Which international restaurant owner is recognized for his advocacy for child adoption?

    A. Carl Karcher
    B. R. Davis Thomas
    C. Cleo R. Ludwig
    D. Norman Brinker

   L.O. 2.

9. Les Dames d'Escoffier is

    A. a bakery/café.
    B. one of the first female-owned restaurants.
    C. a professional organization for women in the restaurant industry.
    D. a theme restaurant where servers wear French costumes.

   L.O. 2.3

10. Alice Waters' restaurant, Chez Panisse became profitable in its

    A. first year.
    B. third year.
    C. eighth year.
    D. tenth year.

   L.O. 2.3

CHAPTER 3

CONCEPT, LOCATION, AND DESIGN

Learning Objectives

After reading this chapter, you should be able to:

3.1   Recognize the benefits of a good restaurant name.

3.2   Explain the relationship between concept and market.

3.3   Explain why a restaurant concept might fail.

3.4   Discuss some qualities of successful restaurant concepts.

3.5   Identify factors to consider when choosing a restaurant's location.

3.6   Identify factors to consider when developing a restaurant concept.

3.7   List restaurant knockout criteria.

Chapter 3 Study Outline

1. Successful foodservice establishments begin with a clear restaurant concept that projects the new restaurant's image. The concept must entice the desired audience in such a way that is different and better than the competition.

2. When choosing a concept, be sure there is a market to support it and a market gap, or need, for the concept offered.

3. The restaurant's name, décor, atmosphere, menu, logo, style of service, and everything else associated with the operation stems from, and should reflect, the original concept.

4. Restaurants have a natural life cycle: birth, growth, maturity, senescence, and death. They often fall into decline due to a change in demographics or when the concept falls out of favor with the public.

5. If a restaurant is failing, adapting the concept to fit the market can often save it.

6. No restaurant concept is completely new, only modified or improved upon from existing operations.

7. A single-concept chain stays with just one successful concept, theme, and niche. A multiple-concept chain profits from several different concepts.

8. Different types of foodservice operations require different levels of service based on many factors, including expected seat turnover rate.

9. Once the concept has been developed, more concrete decisions must be made concerning expected seat turnover rates, space needed per customer, menu prices, marketing strategies, and other aspects of the business.

10. Restaurant owners often write mission statements to solidify for themselves and their employees the company's business goal. It should include:
    - Purpose of the enterprise
    - Business strategy
    - Behavior standards it will follow
    - Values the management and employees will uphold

11. The right location for a restaurant is determined largely by the restaurant's concept. Customers expect quick-service restaurants to be easily accessible, whereas diners looking for a special occasion are more willing to search out the location.

12. The following factors must be evaluated when choosing a site for a restaurant:
    - Demographics of the area: age, occupation, religion, family size, and average income in the community
    - Visibility and accessibility for foot and car traffic
    - Number of potential customers traveling through the area
    - Distance from the potential market
    - Desirability of surroundings

13. Owners must investigate existing and future zoning rules for the site before making a final decision.

14. When any reason is found not to open at a particular site, it is called a knockout criteria. The location should be abandoned in favor of investigating a new one.

15. An excellent way to learn the layout of an area is to use a topographical survey.

16. The décor of a restaurant is critical to its success. The most important aspects are the lighting design and the colors chosen to reflect the restaurant's concept.

Chapter 3 Exercises

1. List five factors that help project a restaurant's concept to its target market.

    - _____

    - _____

    - _____

    - _____

    - _____

L.O. 3.1

2. How can a census tract survey help an owner define a new restaurant's concept and market?

    _____

    _____

    _____

L.O. 3.2

3. Briefly explain why the Victoria Station restaurants failed after years of success. What might the owners have done to save it?

    _____

    _____

    _____

L.O. 3.3

4. Briefly explain the two reasons why Danny Meyer has employees of his Union Square Hospitality group restaurants dine in one of his restaurants every month and write a report about their experiences.

    _____

    _____

    _____

    _____

L.O. 3.4

5. Why might a takeover location be desirable for a new restaurant owner?

_____

_____

_____

L.O. 3.5

6. Why would a fine-dining operation be less concerned about highway access and visibility than a quick-serve restaurant?

_____

_____

_____

L.O. 3.5

7. After watching traffic patterns at a proposed restaurant site, the owner decided to look elsewhere for a place to build his restaurant. List three knockout criteria that affected his decision.

- _____

- _____

- _____

L.O. 3.7

Chapter 3 Check-in

1. To strengthen a restaurant's concept, its name should

   A. be ambiguous.
   B. be the same as the owner's.
   C. immediately establish its identity.
   D. sound a lot like another successful one in the area.

   L.O. 3.1

2. The purpose of developing a restaurant concept is to

   A. determine the break-even point of the business.
   B. reduce employee turnover.
   C. establish inventory-control systems.
   D. define the restaurant's image and target market.

   L.O. 3.2

3. The concept for a new restaurant should

   A. always be completely new.
   B. copy and improve on an existing restaurant.
   C. replicate exactly a successful chain restaurant.
   D. always include merchandising tie-ins to increase profits.

L.O. 3.2

4. Which of the following factors most often leads to the decline of a successful restaurant?

   A. Major change in demographics
   B. Introduction of a new concept
   C. Increase in costs
   D. Hiring inexperienced servers

L.O. 3.3

5. The logo, service uniforms, and types of napkins are all examples of a restaurant's

   A. mission.
   B. hiring policy.
   C. symbology.
   D. character.

L.O. 3.4

6. A well-written mission statement helps

   A. focus energies of management and employees.
   B. customers know what type of service to expect.
   C. reduce labor costs.
   D. managers develop job specifications.

L.O. 3.4

7. This type of restaurant is most concerned about visibility.

   A. Quick-service operation
   B. Dinner house
   C. Steakhouse
   D. Fine-dining establishment

L.O. 3.5

8. Which of the following traffic generators would be most favorable for a fine-dining establishment?

   A. Business park
   B. Major freeway interchange
   C. Nearby lake or stream
   D. Sports arena

L.O. 3.5

9. A topographical survey helps a restaurateur determine

   A. if a proposed site is zoned for a restaurant.
   B. the distance of a proposed site to the nearest highway.
   C. how many cars can fit in the parking lot.
   D. the number of similar restaurants in a given area.

L.O. 3.7

10. When a restaurant lease is only available for less than five years, most proposed owners would consider it a(n)

   A. bargain.
   B. incentive to become profitable quickly.
   C. knockout criteria.
   D. standard lease and expect to renegotiate later.

L.O. 3.7

CHAPTER 4

RESTAURANT BUSINESS AND MARKETING PLANS

Learning Objectives

After reading this chapter, you should be able to:

4.1   Identify the major elements of a business plan.

4.2   Develop a restaurant business plan.

4.3   Conduct a market assessment.

4.4   Discuss the importance of the four Ps of the marketing mix.

4.5   Describe some promotional ideas for a restaurant.

Chapter 4 Study Outline

1. A business plan helps determine the potential success of a restaurant. It is also used to obtain financing.

2. It is necessary to determine benefits the restaurant provides customers that are not offered by competitors, and then communicate this advantage to attract potential customers.

3. To determine and promote a restaurant's competitive advantage, managers should develop a marketing strategy based on the four Ps.

    *   Price—should be within the range expected by the target market, but still high enough to remain profitable.

    *   Product—excellent food, service, and atmosphere that meets the demands of the target market.

    *   Place—must be visible, accessible, and convenient.

    *   Promotion—communicating the benefits the restaurant offers to the target market through advertising.

4. Regardless of the type of advertising a restaurant chooses to use, it must be appropriate for the target market and induce customers to visit the restaurant often.

Chapter 4 Exercises

1. What are the two most important reasons for writing a business plan?

    • _____

    • _____

L.O. 4.1

2. Match the following terms with their meaning:

    _____(1)   Marketing plan
    _____(2)   Marketing strategy
    _____(3)   Market assessment
    _____(4)   Market potential

    a. Defines the number of customers, near or far, that might visit the restaurant
    b. Contains realistic objectives for sales and costs while leaving a reasonable profit
    c. Analyzes the community, customers, and competition
    d. Positions the restaurant in relation to its competition

L.O. 4.3

3. Are the following activities advertising (A), public relations (PR), or promotions (P)?

    _____a. Purchasing space in a local newspaper
    _____b. Appearing on a national talk show to demonstrate cooking techniques
    _____c. Donating dinner for four to a charity auction
    _____d. Handing out food samples at a community festival
    _____e. Paying for the uniforms of a local soccer team
    _____f. Judging the pie-baking contest at the county fair
    _____g. Mailing two-for-one coupons to senior citizens
    _____h. Putting two-for-one coupons in the local newspaper
    _____i. Organizing a food drive for a nearby homeless shelter
    _____j. Announcing a new menu item on the radio

L.O. 4.4

Chapter 4 Check-in

1. The analysis that determines the
    potential profitability of a restaurant
    concept is called a

    A. market assessment.
    B. business plan.
    C. business review.
    D. market demand.

    L.O. 4.1

2. In foodservice, marketing focuses on
    the needs of the

    A. servers.
    B. guests.
    C. owners.
    D. investors.

    L.O. 4.3

3. This is used to assess the strengths
    and weaknesses of other restaurants
    in the area.

    A. Market demand
    B. Marketing strategy
    C. Competition analysis
    D. Market potential

    L.O. 4.3

4. Which of the following is a marketing
    strategy?

    A. Increase the number of guests by
        ten percent.
    B. Raise the price for fried chicken.
    C. Mail coupons to existing
        customers.
    D. Purchase an advertisement in a
        local newspaper.

    L.O. 4.3

5. An analysis of the community, the
    customers, and the competition is a

    A. marketing strategy.
    B. business plan.
    C. market segmentation.
    D. market assessment.

    L.O. 4.3

6. An organization's emphasis on the
    freshness of its ingredients is an
    example of

    A. corporate buying power.
    B. ordering skills.
    C. product positioning.
    D. superior employee training
        programs.

    L.O. 4.3

7. Combining complementary
    restaurants under one roof uses which
    of the four Ps of the marketing mix?

    A. Place
    B. Product
    C. Price
    D. Promotion

    L.O. 4.4

8. Product analysis examines the

    A. amount of fresh fruit and
        vegetables ordered by the chef.
    B. income level of the people who
        live in the target market.
    C. restaurant's visibility from
        the street.
    D. quality, pricing, and degree of
        service offered by a restaurant.

    L.O. 4.4

9. Basing menu-item prices on those set by other area restaurants is an example of

    A. cost-based pricing.
    B. competitive pricing.
    C. contribution pricing.
    D. price fixing.

    L.O. 4.4

10. An example of a loss-leader meal is

    A. a two-for-one dinner coupon.
    B. a donation to a local homeless shelter.
    C. removing a menu item that is not selling well.
    D. paying for a customer's taxi ride home.

    L.O. 4.5

CHAPTER 5

FINANCING AND LEASING

Learning Objectives

After reading this chapter, you should be able to:

5.1   Forecast restaurant sales.

5.2   Prepare an income statement.

5.3   Prepare a financial budget.

5.4   Identify requirements for obtaining a loan in order to start a restaurant.

5.5   Discuss the strengths and weaknesses of the various types of loans available to restaurant operators.

5.6   List questions and the types of clauses a lessee should consider before signing a lease.

Chapter 5 Study Outline

1. Though poor management might be cited as the reason for a restaurant failure, insufficient financing and a shortage of working capital may also play major roles in an operation's demise.

2. It is not necessary to own the entire restaurant. Experienced owners often rent or lease the land and building, then secure financing to purchase equipment and have access to working capital.

3. Before approaching investors, owners must prepare a budget based on projected sales and operational costs. Creating this budget requires forecasting of:

    - Sales
    - Cost of sales
    - Budgeted costs
    - Controllable expenses
    - Pre-opening expenses

4. Sales volume is determined by two factors:

    - Average guest check—what each patron spends

- Guest count—number of customers over a specific period of time

5. Costs are divided into two categories:
   - Fixed costs remain the same regardless of business volume and sales. These include real estate taxes, depreciation on equipment, and insurance.
   - Variable costs change proportionately according to sales. Food and beverage costs go up or down depending on sales volume. The rent may also increase if sales exceed a predetermined amount stated in the lease.

6. Controllable expenses are those management can manipulate. They include payroll, direct operating expenses, and marketing.

7. Operators can borrow capital from a bank, savings and loan, private lenders, limited partners, or the Small Business Association (SBA).

8. Securing an SBA loan is a four-step process that requires:
   - Obtaining a list of participating banks
   - Submitting a completed applications to a member bank
   - Waiting for the local SBA to approve the loan
   - Visiting the lender to sign the loan documents

9. Lenders want to see a thorough business plan that assures funds will be put to work as soon as capital becomes available.

10. The borrower must have collateral, or hard assets, to secure a loan. Lenders will also evaluate a prospective borrower's character to determine his/her creditworthiness.

11. New restaurant owners may choose to lease the building and equipment because it requires less capital. However, if the business fails before the lease expires, the owner is still responsible for all outstanding lease payments.

12. When drawing up a lease agreement, a number of critical issues must be addressed. Among the most important are:
    - Amount of lease payment and how it is paid
    - Which equipment is included in the lease
    - Who is responsible for repair and maintenance of the equipment and facilities
    - Who pays the common-area maintenance costs
    - Duration of the lease
    - Which party is responsible for carrying fire insurance

Chapter 5 Exercises

1. Many restaurants fail because the owners do not have sufficient _____ _____ to keep it running long enough to build a customer base.
   L.O. 5.1

2. Instead of buying the building and land, some owners conserve their finances by either _____ or _____ them.
   L.O. 5.1

3. To reduce their risk, asset lenders expect owners to pledge _____ in case the loan is not repaid.
   L.O. 5.1

4. List the two factors used to forecast sales in a new restaurant.

   • _____

   • _____

   L.O. 5.1

5. Real estate taxes and insurance premiums are examples of _____ costs.
   L.O. 5.2

6. Payroll, marketing, and general repairs are examples of _____ costs.
   L.O. 5.3

7. The three principal parties involved in an SBA-guaranteed loan are the _____, the _____ _____ _____, and the _____ _____.

   L.O. 5.4

8. Most loans rejected by the SBA are due to financial information that is _____ _____.

   L.O. 5.4

9. SBA loan applications can be obtained, completed, and returned to a _____ _____.

   L.O. 5.4

10. The document that shows a lender that a borrower is capable of running a successful restaurant is a _____.

L.O. 5.4

11. List three things lenders scrutinize to determine an applicant's character.

- _____

- _____

- _____

L.O. 5.4

12. List three assets banks often accept as collateral for a loan.

- _____

- _____

- _____

L.O. 5.4

13. In addition to family, friends, and banks, what are three other sources of financing?

- _____

- _____

- _____

L.O. 5.5

14. What are the three owner expenses meant by the term CAMs?

- _____

- _____

- _____

L.O. 5.6

15. One clause in the lease should state that the lease is void if what cannot be obtained?

_____

L.O. 5.6

Chapter 5 Check-in

1. The best way to convince investors and lenders to support a new restaurant is to
   - A. advertise in the business section of the local newspaper.
   - B. write a business plan.
   - C. join the local chamber of commerce.
   - D. take bankers to lunch at a restaurant similar to the one you want to open.

   L.O. 5.1

2. This shows the profitability of a restaurant over a given period of time.
   - A. Income statement
   - B. Sales forecast
   - C. Productivity analysis
   - D. Personal financial statement

   L.O. 5.2

3. Which of the following is a controllable expense?
   - A. Collateral
   - B. Real estate taxes
   - C. Insurance payments
   - D. Payroll

   L.O. 5.3

4. Which of the following is a fixed asset?
   - A. Cash
   - B. Accounts receivable
   - C. Furniture
   - D. Inventory

   L.O. 5.3

5. Lenders reduce their monetary risk by requiring borrowers to pledge
   - A. allegiance.
   - B. a percentage of future profits.
   - C. collateral.
   - D. the good faith value of the business

   L.O. 5.4

6. After completing an application for an SBA loan, it is first reviewed by
   - A. the IRS.
   - B. a commercial lender.
   - C. the SBA
   - D. the USDA

   L.O. 5.4

7. Lenders believe this is the most important form of collateral.
   - A. Real estate
   - B. Life insurance
   - C. Savings accounts
   - D. Personal character

   L.O. 5.4

8. A borrower who may need a loan in the future can stockpile credit by
   - A. using a large number of credit cards.
   - B. refinancing a home mortgage.
   - C. compiling the necessary financial paperwork and information in draft form.
   - D. opening a line a credit at a local bank.

   L.O. 5.4

9. A lease agreement that passes the cost of upkeep and tax increases to the restaurant operator is called a
   A. term loan.
   B. condemnation clause.
   C. triple-net lease.
   D. pass-through investment.

L.O. 5.6

10. A restaurant owner should ask for a cotenancy clause if
    A. it is located in a shopping center that might lose an anchor tenant.
    B. the owner expects to expand menu offerings in the future.
    C. the owner might need to sublet a portion of the restaurant.
    D. real estate taxes are expected to rise soon.

L.O. 5.6

CHAPTER 6

LEGAL AND TAX MATTERS

Learning Objectives

After reading this chapter, you should be able to:

6.1 Describe the various forms of business ownership.

6.2 Discuss the advantages and disadvantages of each form of business.

6.3 Recognize the legal aspects of doing business.

Chapter 6 Study Outline

1. Every foodservice owner/operator must decide what type of business organization is best for his/her enterprise.

2. All businesses are seen legally as proprietorships, partnerships, or corporations, each with its own unique tax consequences that affect the following:

   - Federal income taxes

   - Liability to creditors

   - Legal and/or personal relationships among owners

   - Legal life and transfer of ownership in the future

3. A sole proprietorship is the simplest way to form a business organization. Owners are not treated as employees for tax purposes. Their income is based solely on profits from the enterprise. However, they must pay self-employment taxes.

4. A partnership accommodates several owners.

   - In a general partnership, all members share in the management and liabilities of the company.

   - In a limited partnership (often called a silent partnership), one or more parties have limited liability but no decision-making powers.

   - Partnership income taxes are similar to those of sole proprietorships.

5. Corporations allow individuals to separate their personal assets from the business.

6. Additional funds can be raised by selling stock in the corporation, but to remain in control the owner must retain fifty-one percent of the company's stock.

7. Because it is considered a separate legal entity, a corporation is taxed on its earned income. Owners paid either a salary or dividends from the company are then taxed again.

8. To avoid double taxation, some owners choose to file as an S corporation. This is also a smart way to offset operating losses in the first few years of business.

9. After choosing the right type of business organization, owners must still meet and/or obtain a long list of requirements, permits, and licenses before opening their doors to customers. Among the most important are:

   - Zoning ordinances governing how and where a business can locate
   - Local and state health-code regulations, which establish the standards every operation must meet
   - Business licenses and tax registration
   - Workers' compensation insurance
   - Federal workplace laws governing safety precautions and benefits given to employees

10. To maximize cash flow, many restaurants use an accelerated depreciation method because it reduces taxes during the first years of the business.

11. Restaurant owners can deduct a number of expenses from their taxes, including:

    - Attending industry-related meetings and conventions
    - Company-owned car
    - Life and health insurance for executives and their families

12. All businesses with more than one employee must file with the IRS, obtain an employer identification number, and withhold federal payroll taxes.

13. It is very important for business owners to familiarize themselves with all federal regulations governing employment. These laws mandate not only the number of hours a week an employee can work, but also mandate that discrimination based on race, sex, or age is illegal.

Chapter 6 Exercises

1. List three types of restaurant business organizations.

   - _____

   - _____

   - _____

L.O. 6.1

2. What are some of the advantages and disadvantages of operating a restaurant as a sole proprietor?

_____

_____

_____

L.O. 6.2

3. Briefly explain how restaurants operating as corporations are double taxed, and explain what owners can do to avoid this situation.

_____

_____

_____

L.O. 6.2

4. Why might a new restaurant owner choose an accelerated depreciation method?

_____

_____

_____

L.O. 6.3

5. Indicate whether the following statements are true (T) or false (F).

_____a. The cost for attending a restaurant trade show is fully deductible.

_____b. Anyone who works more than forty hours in a single week must be paid overtime for extra work.

_____c. Sixteen-year-olds must have a work permit in order to operate a food slicer.

_____d. The Federal Equal Pay Act prohibits employers from discriminating on the basis of age or race.

_____e. The most effective way to prevent sexual harassment is the adoption and dissemination of a sexual harassment policy.

_____f. It is the responsibility of a server to reprimand a customer who makes sexual advances.

_____g. Federal laws make it illegal to hire anyone under the age of fourteen.

_____h. As long as they do not serve food, musicians are always considered contract employees by the law.

_____i. A liquor license can be withdrawn by the Alcoholic Beverage Commission if a restaurant owner fails to comply with regulations.

_____j. If a server sells alcohol to a minor, the only person prosecuted will be the restaurant owner.

L.O. 6.3

Chapter 6 Check-in

1. Restaurant owners often choose to operate as a sole proprietorship because
   A. it is the least complicated business entity.
   B. the business automatically transfers to heirs if the owner dies.
   C. it reduces the owner's social security taxes.
   D. the owner is automatically covered by the company's medical insurance.

L.O. 6.1

2. The disadvantage of this type of business entity is the possibility of double taxation.
   A. Sole proprietorship
   B. Partnership
   C. Corporation
   D. S corporation

L.O. 6.2

3. In which business entity can available funds be withdrawn without tax consequences?
   A. Sole proprietorship
   B. Partnership
   C. Corporation
   D. S corporation

L.O. 6.2

4. For tax purposes, which of the following is a nondepreciable item?
   A. Kitchen equipment
   B. The restaurant building
   C. The land
   D. Dining-room furniture

L.O. 6.3

5. New restaurant owners often choose accelerated-depreciation methods in order to
   A. sell their used equipment sooner.
   B. simplify their tax filing.
   C. increase available cash.
   D. look more profitable to investors.

L.O. 6.3

6. The best way to prevent a sexual harassment lawsuit is to
   A. adopt a sexual harassment policy and educate employees about it.
   B. tell employees to refer complaints to the national office.
   C. let employees work it out among themselves.
   D. hire only married employees.

L.O. 6.3

7. How long will it take an investment of $10,000 at 10% interest to double in value?

    A. 5.5 years
    B. 7.2 years
    C. 10.5 years
    D. 12 years

    L.O. 6.3

8. Workers' Compensation Insurance is administered by

    A. the federal government.
    B. the local government.
    C. the state government.
    D. private insurers.

    L.O. 6.3

9. How old must an employee be to operate a food slicer?

    A. 14
    B. 16
    C. 18
    D. 21

    L.O. 6.3

10. Restaurants are sued most often when

    A. customers are refused service.
    B. customers slip and fall.
    C. customers are overcharged.
    D. underaged customers are served alcohol.

    L.O. 6.3

CHAPTER 7

THE MENU

Learning Objectives

After reading this chapter, you should be able to:

7.1   Identify factors to consider when planning a menu.

7.2   List and describe some common menu types.

7.3   Discuss methods for determining menu item pricing.

7.4   Identify factors to consider when determining a menu's design and layout.

Chapter 7 Study Outline

1.   The menu is the controlling document in all foodservice operations. Designing the menu is the highest priority when opening a new restaurant. The menu must satisfy or exceed guests' expectations because the restaurant concept is based on what the target market expects.

2.   When planning a new menu, managers must be aware of how each choice will affect different aspects of the restaurant. Choices must be matched with the following:

   * Capabilities of the chef
   * Equipment to be used
   * Availability of ingredients
   * Customers' price/value perceptions
   * Nutritional needs of patrons
   * Contribution margins of each menu item
   * Flavors the target market will find intriguing

3.   A table d'hote menu allows patrons to build a complete meal at a fixed price.

4.   Appetizers, soups, salads, entrées, and desserts normally are given their own sections in the menu. Coffee shops often devote a separate section for breakfast food, even if they are served all day long.

5.   After all selections have been made, a menu analysis should be conducted to show a balance between items with a high food cost percentage and those with a low food cost percentage.

6. The layout, format, and paper type of a menu must match its operation's décor and theme.

7. Chefs and kitchen staff follow standardized recipes to maintain consistent food quality.

8. An operation's cost of goods consumed is found using the following formula: *Opening inventory + Purchases – Closing inventory = Cost of food consumed.*

9. Food cost percentage is the guideline most owners use to determine their profitability. The food cost percentage is determined by using the following formula: *Cost of goods sold ÷ Total sales = Food-cost percentage.*

Chapter 7 Exercises

1. List two of the major challenges a restaurant owner faces when planning a new menu.

   • _____

   • _____

L.O. 7.1

2. Why is the menu considered so important to the success of a restaurant?

_____

_____

_____

L.O. 7.1

3. How can a restaurant ensure all menu items have the right weight, shape, and taste, as described in the menu?

_____

_____

_____

L.O. 7.1

4. In what ways are restaurants trying to meet the increasing demand for more nutritious menu items?

_____

_____

_____

L.O. 7.1

5. When restaurants are short on kitchen space, what items are often purchased off site?

_____

_____

_____

L.O. 7.1

6. Customers often consider this more important than service, value, or cleanliness.

_____

L.O. 7.1

7. Why do some restaurant owners prefer seasonal menus?

_____

_____

_____

L.O. 7.2

8. What are the two basic components of value creation?

- _____

- _____

L.O. 7.3

9. The difference between the sales of an item and its cost is called what?

_____

L.O. 7.3

10. What should be done when the price of a menu item must be increased drastically?

_____

_____

_____

L.O. 7.3

11. Where is the focal point of a single-page menu?

_____

L.O. 7.4

12. Why should the owner of a new restaurant print a variety of inexpensive menus?

_____

_____

_____

L.O. 7.4

13. Describe the method for calculating the cost of food consumed.

_____

_____

_____

L.O. 7.4

14. How is the food cost percentage determined?

_____

_____

_____

L.O. 7.4

Chapter 7 Check-in

1. Patrons consider this the most important factor when choosing a restaurant.

    A. Location
    B. Parking
    C. Food quality
    D. Price

    L.O. 7.1

2. When choosing menu items, doing this first will better position the restaurant.

    A. Hiring high-profile chefs
    B. Researching popular recipes
    C. Developing standardized recipes
    D. Analyzing competing restaurants

    L.O. 7.1

3. What is likely to happen if too many menu items require the same kitchen equipment for preparation?

   A. Guests will grow tired of the menu.
   B. Production will slow down.
   C. Kitchen staff will grow bored of their jobs.
   D. Food quality will suffer.

   L.O. 7.1

4. Health-minded consumers are most concerned with a food item's

   A. sodium content.
   B. fat content.
   C. cholesterol.
   D. omega-3 content.

   L.O. 7.1

5. Why are more menu-item descriptions using terms like marinated and smoked?

   A. To abide by truth-in-labeling laws
   B. To let guests know their food was handled safely
   C. To promote new and interesting flavors
   D. Because fewer chefs are using heavy sauces

   L.O. 7.1

6. When waiting on children, servers should

   A. bend over and make eye contact with them.
   B. join them as they color on their placemats.
   C. push them to try new food items.
   D. delay coming by until they are quiet.

   L.O. 7.2

7. This type of menu is a sample of the chef's best dishes.

   A. La grande cuisine française
   B. À la carte
   C. Table d'hôte
   D. Degustation

   L.O. 7.2

8. This type of menu is a selection of several dishes served at a fixed price.

   A. La grande cuisine française
   B. À la carte
   C. Table d'hôte
   D. Degustation

   L.O. 7.2

9. One way to increase profits without raising prices is to

   A. reduce portion sizes.
   B. offer two-for-one coupons.
   C. stop offering free refills on drinks.
   D. share tips with servers.

   L.O. 7.3

10. Images or graphics are added to menus in order to

    A. fill the white space.
    B. help non-English speaking customers order.
    C. increase sales of a particular item.
    D. win awards.

    L.O. 7.4

CHAPTER 8

BAR AND BEVERAGES

Learning Objectives

After reading this chapter, students should be able to:

8.1   Explain how to obtain an alcoholic beverage license.

8.2   Identify factors to consider when developing the design and layout of a bar.

8.3   List guidelines for suggesting wines to accompany menu items.

8.4   Identify a restaurant's legal liability regarding the sale of alcoholic beverages.

8.5   List ways in which bartenders and others can defraud the restaurant bar and beverage operation.

Chapter 8 Study Outline

1.   Each state has its own department of alcoholic beverage control (ABC), which regulates the manufacture, importing, and sale of all alcoholic beverages in that state.

2.   There are two basic types of liquor licenses: a general license for all alcohol sales and another for serving beer and wine only.

3.   To receive a new license, both the ABC and local governments must approve the application.

4.   Once the license is obtained, all liquor must be purchased from either a wholesaler or manufacturer.

5.   The bar setup is divided into three areas:
      (1) Front bar, where guests may sit and where the bartender mixes drinks
      (2) Back bar, which may be designed for aesthetics and to hold additional liquor
      (3) Under bar, where main equipment, such as the speed rack, is located

6.   The design for a new bar will depend on the restaurant's concept—whether the bar will be a major retail area or a holding zone for guests waiting to be seated.

7.   Selecting the right bartender is critical to the success of a bar because it is the bartender's responsibility to manage the operation and ensure that all liquor laws are followed.

8.   The two most important qualities to consider when choosing the appropriate wine are richness and body.

9. Flavor and texture describe both food and wine, so light wines should be matched with light food.

10. Both the nose and the tongue determine flavor.

11. Developing and maintaining a responsible alcohol-service program is of vital importance. If a problem with a patron does occur, be sure to document the situation.

12. Dram shop laws state that owners of drinking establishments are responsible for injuries caused by intoxicated customers.

13. The penalty for serving alcohol to minors or intoxicated customers is severe and can be imposed on both the server and the owner of the restaurant or bar.

14. To avoid loss of alcohol through mishandling or theft, a weekly or biweekly audit should be conducted.

15. Restaurant owners must remain aware of the vast number of ways theft can occur in their establishments. Putting control systems in place will discourage most employees from theft and will make catching the percentage of employees who do steal much easier.

Chapter 8 Exercises

1. Indicate whether the following statements are True (T) or False (F).

_____a.   A license issued by the ABC is not a right, but a privilege that can be revoked.

_____b.   All liquor licenses allow owners to sell distilled spirits off site.

_____c.   In California, liquor licenses can be sold only within the county.

_____d.   When purchasing an existing restaurant, the license is automatically transferred to the new owner.

_____e.   Owners of liquor licenses can purchase alcohol only from a wholesaler or manufacturer.

L.O. 8.1

_____f.   The section where customers sit to order drinks is called the front bar.

_____g.   Merlot, Cabernet Sauvignon, and Zinfandel are popular red wines.

_____h.   Champagne should only be served with appetizers or desserts.

_____i.   Wines should be chosen for their richness and body.

_____j.   Red wine should never be served with pork.

_____k.   It is best to pour white wine with vinegary salads because it is served colder than red wine.

L.O. 8.2, 8.3

_____l. Developing a responsible alcohol-service program eliminates the possibility of alcohol-abuse lawsuits.

_____m. Under the dram shop laws, drinking establishment owners are liable for injuries caused by intoxicated customers.

_____n. One way to reduce theft of alcohol is to institute a weekly audit.

L.O. 8.4

2. List three ways to control losses from the bar area.

- _____

- _____

- _____

L.O. 8.5

Chapter 8 Check-in

1. Licenses to sell alcoholic beverages are overseen by the
    A. local zoning council.
    B. county sheriff's department.
    C. executive branch of each state.
    D. federal government.
    L.O. 8. 1

2. Liquor-license owners can purchase alcohol only from
    A. grocery stores.
    B. the department of alcoholic beverage control.
    C. liquor stores.
    D. wholesalers or manufacturers.
    L.O. 8.1

3. In a bar layout, the speed rack
    A. displays extra bottles.
    B. allows the bartender to quickly make drinks.
    C. dries glassware quickly.
    D. dispenses mixers automatically.
    L.O. 8.2

4. The pouring device that dispenses colas, juices, and other mixers is called a
    A. speed gun.
    B. speed rack.
    C. bar back.
    D. mixer-dispenser.
    L.O. 8.2

5. The person in the bar area in charge of taking cash is
    A. the bartender.
    B. the cocktail waitress.
    C. the hostess.
    D. any available server.
    L.O. 8.2

6. When pairing wines with food, champagne is
    A. best served with white meats.
    B. best served with red meats.
    C. fine throughout the meal.
    D. only served with dessert.
    L.O. 8.3

36

7. Which of the following types of wine should be chilled before serving?

    A. Merlot
    B. Sauvignon Blanc
    C. Pinot Noir
    D. Zinfandel

    L.O. 8.3

8. A strong defense against an alcohol-related lawsuit is to

    A. obtain a liquor license.
    B. write a responsible alcohol-service mission statement.
    C. know the design of each state's driver's licenses.
    D. hire off-duty police officers as bouncers.

    L.O. 8.4

9. Rules governing the sale of alcoholic beverages to minors or intoxicated people are overseen by the

    A. federal child labor department.
    B. U. S. Department of Agriculture.
    C. Mothers Against Drunk Driving.
    D. dram shop laws.

    L.O. 8.4

10. To reduce the accidental loss or theft of alcohol, many restaurants conduct

    A. lie detector tests.
    B. drug abuse analysis.
    C. weekly audits.
    D. wine-tasting seminars.

    L.O. 8.5

CHAPTER 9

FOOD PURCHASING

Learning Objectives

After reading this chapter, students should be able to:

9.1   Explain the importance of product specifications.

9.2   List and describe the steps for creating a purchasing system.

9.3   Identify factors to consider when establishing par stocks and reordering points.

9.4   Explain selection factors for purchasing meat, produce, canned goods, coffee, and other items.

Chapter 9 Study Outline

1. Once in place, an effective food-purchasing system will help the entire restaurant run smoothly. To work properly, it must establish:
    - Product specifications
    - Method to control effort and losses
    - Par stocks and reorder points for all items
    - Person in charge of the ordering process
    - Person responsible for accepting and storing all deliveries

2. Product specifications tell suppliers exactly what characteristics are required for each food item ordered by the restaurant.

3. Maintaining a close relationship with a few key suppliers reduces ordering time and can lead to advance warnings of pending price increases or scarcity of availability.

4. To determine when to order inventory items and how much to order, managers must forecast business volume. They then set a par stock (the minimum amount that should be on hand at any given time) and a reorder point (a time to place a new order based on the amount in stock) for every item in the inventory.

5. At large restaurants, orders are generally placed in the form of a purchase order listing the items to be delivered.

6. A standing order is often used for perishable items, such as milk or bread, which is delivered automatically at regular intervals.

7. To ensure product quality and cost control, each item must be stored in a proper location, maintained at the proper temperature, and issued before the end of its shelf life.

8. Most operations use the first-in, first-out (FIFO) issuing method in which older items are used before newly delivered items.

9. Buying from a full-line purveyor provides one-stop shopping, reducing ordering, and receiving time.

10. Meat items are chosen for their grade, which are determined by the USDA and based on fat content, tenderness, and cost.

11. The quality of meat needed for each restaurant depends on the restaurant's concept.

12. Meat can be purchased as a whole carcass, wholesale cut, or in ready-to-serve portions.

13. To receive the quality of fresh fruit and vegetables that is right for the restaurant, the buyer must specify the grade, size, count, container size, and degree of ripeness. The USDA has set federal standards that help when making buying decisions.

14. Operators who use canned fruit or vegetables frequently should conduct can-cutting tests in the late fall to compare the quality of various vendors.

15. Coffee flavors vary greatly and depend on where the beans were grown and how long they were roasted. The choice is based on the clients' expectations. Some coffee manufacturers will install a brewing machine if the owner promises to order all the coffee from that manufacturer.

Chapter 9 Exercises

1. List the five factors that must be determined to develop a food-purchasing system.

   - _____
   - _____
   - _____
   - _____
   - _____

L.O. 9.2

2. Why are more restaurant owners purchasing goods with only a few select purveyors?

   _____
   _____
   _____

L.O. 9.2

3. How does the manager ensure the right quality of food is delivered to the restaurant?

_____

_____

_____

L.O. 9.2

4. What is the difference between par stock and the reorder point?

_____

_____

_____

L.O. 9.3

5. Why do purchasers hold annual can-cutting tests?

_____

_____

_____

L.O. 9.4

6. Managers often request daily price quotes for what types of food?

_____

_____

_____

L.O. 9.4

7. What stock-rotation system do most restaurants use to minimize spoilage in their storerooms?

_____

_____

_____

L.O. 9.4

8. What are the three principle factors meat buyers use to make purchasing decisions?

- _____

- _____

- _____

L.O. 9.4

9. List two ways restaurants can minimize costs while still offering fresh fruit.

- _____

- _____

L.O. 9.4

10. How can a new restaurant owner reduce the cost of coffee?

_____

_____

_____

L.O. 9.4

Chapter 9 Check-in

1. A detailed description of a food item is called a
   A. standing order.
   B. par stock number.
   C. food-quality standard.
   D. product specification.
   L.O. 9.1

2. When developing a purchasing system, the par stock is the
   A. general term for all canned goods.
   B. reasonable amount of an item to have on hand at all times.
   C. most of any one item that should be on hand.
   D. moment when more should be ordered.
   L.O. 9.2

3. In most restaurants, the person in charge of setting up the purchasing system is the
   A. owner.
   B. manager.
   C. chef.
   D. person who receives and stores deliveries.
   L.O. 9.2

4. A predetermined order that is filled regularly is called a
   A. purchase order.
   B. reorder point.
   C. standing order.
   D. convenience delivery.
   L.O. 9.2

5. Purchasing from this type of distributor can reduce costs because it charges only enough of a markup to cover its costs.

    A. Full-line purveyors
    B. Cooperatives
    C. Specialty food processors
    D. Farmers' markets

L.O. 9.2

6. The government agency that oversees the sale of meat is the

    A. USDA.
    B. U.S. Department of Commerce.
    C. U.S. Department of the Interior.
    D. FDA.

L.O. 9.4

7. Fruit- and vegetable-grade standards are determined by the

    A. USDA.
    B. U.S. Department of Commerce.
    C. U.S. Department of the Interior.
    D. FDA.

L.O. 9.4

8. The quality standards and fill requirements of canned goods are established by the

    A. USDA.
    B. U.S. Department of Commerce.
    C. U.S. Department of the Interior.
    D. FDA.

L.O. 9.4

9. Foodservice operators often conduct can-cutting tests to determine

    A. the freshness of the restaurant's canned goods.
    B. the sharpness of the prep kitchen's can opener.
    C. the quality of that season's canned goods.
    D. if they can use canned goods that have passed their "sell-by" dates.

L.O. 9.4

10. It is best to buy coffee that is

    A. mountain grown.
    B. expensive.
    C. right for the target market.
    D. the most popular brand.

L.O. 9.4

CHAPTER 10

PLANNING AND EQUIPPING THE KITCHEN

Learning Objectives

After reading this chapter, students should be able to:

10.1   Identify factors to consider when planning a kitchen's layout.

10.2   Explain selection factors for purchasing kitchen equipment.

Chapter 10 Study Outline

1. A well-designed kitchen will do the following:

    - Minimize the number of steps taken by wait staff and kitchen personnel

    - Accommodate the needs of workers and customers who are disabled, as mandated by federal regulations

    - Meet the sanitary guidelines established by the National Sanitation Foundation

2. The most effective kitchen plan is rectangular in shape.

3. Open kitchens allow customers to observe the chef in action, but are more expensive to build because they require both an interesting piece of equipment on which to focus, and acoustical tile to reduce noise from the kitchen.

4. Kitchen floors should be made with materials that are nonabsorbent, easy to clean, and resistant to harsh chemicals.

5. Equipment is a major expense and investment for any foodservice owner, so its selection and maintenance is crucial. Equipment is selected to meet the operation's production needs, capacity of its staff, and financial resources.

6. All foodservice managers should be familiar with common pieces of equipment found in various areas of the operation.

    - Reach-in refrigerator and freezer (storage area)

    - Walk-in refrigerator and freezer (storage area)

    - Ice machines (storage area)

    - Mixer (prepreparation area)

    - Slicer (prepreparation area)

    - Peeler (prepreparation area)

- Range (cooking area)
- Deep-fryer (cooking area)
- Grill (cooking area)
- Ovens (cooking area)
- Steamer (cooking area)
- Broiler (cooking area)
- Food warmer (service and holding area)
- Steam table (service and holding area)
- Toaster (service and holding area)
- Dishwasher (clean-up area)
- Garbage disposer (clean-up area)

7. Several types of ovens are used in foodservice: low-temperature, forced-air convection, microwave, and infrared.

8. Not all equipment needs be bought new. Used equipment with a long life ahead of it can be found, reducing costs.

9. All equipment must be cleaned and maintained regularly to ensure its longest life. This is especially true of the dishwasher, which requires constant maintenance. If it breaks down, not only will there be a short supply of dishware, but repairs often require waiting for a specialist to arrive. Some restaurants lease the dishwasher, leaving maintenance problems to the dishwasher's owner.

10. Whether a restaurant is newly constructed or replacing an existing restaurant, it must pass inspections by public health officials and local planning boards before the public can enter.

Chapter 10 Exercises

1. The basic goal of kitchen planning is to keep _____ _____ to a minimum.

L.O. 10.1

2. The most efficient kitchen layout is _____ in shape.

L.O. 10.1

3. Regardless of a kitchen designer's best intentions, servers will establish traffic patterns that are the _____.

L.O. 10.1

4. Open kitchens are more expensive to operate because they require an interesting focal point and the instillation of _____ _____ to reduce noise.

L.O. 10.1

5. The most frequent cause of kitchen accidents is _____ and _____.
L.O. 10.1

6. When filled with water, _____ - _____ _____ can be used to blanch vegetables.
L.O. 10.2

7. _____ _____ use a fan or rotor to circulate air rapidly to heat food quicker than conventional ovens.
L.O. 10.2

8. The one piece of kitchen equipment that must be constantly maintained is the _____ _____. L.O. 10.2

9. Prior to opening, a restaurant must pass an examination by the local _____ _____.

L.O. 10.2

10. Match each piece of equipment with the kitchen area where it is normally found. Note that some letters will be used more than once. L.O. 10.2

_____(1) Disposer

_____(2) Can opener

_____(3) Coffee maker

_____(4) Refrigerator

_____(5) Steamer

_____(6) Range

_____(7) Dishwasher

_____(8) Griddle

_____(9) Salamander

_____(10) Infrared lamp

a. Storage
b. Prepreparation
c. Cooking
d. Serving
e. Cleanup and sanitation

Chapter 10 Check-in

1. Which kitchen work-flow diagram wastes space in the center of the room?

   A. Rectangular
   B. Square
   C. Oval
   D. Circular

   L.O. 10.1

2. Managers should enforce rules that require all spills be picked up immediately in order to

   A. pass a surprise health inspection.
   B. keep the open kitchen's appearance at its best.
   C. avoid a bad review from a local food critic.
   D. prevent people from slipping and falling.

   L.O. 10.1

3. The preparation technique in which individual servings are vacuum packed and refrigerated for future use is called

   A. sous vide.
   B. cook-chill.
   C. à la carte.
   D. de-skilling.

   L.O. 10.2

4. This type of stove can cook different foods at different temperatures at the same time.

   A. Rangetop stove
   B. Sectionalized griddle
   C. Grooved griddle
   D. Broiler

   L.O. 10.2

5. One way to reduce meat shrinkage during cooking is to use a

   A. microwave oven.
   B. low-temperature oven.
   C. convection oven.
   D. deep-fat fryer.

   L.O. 10.2

6. Restaurants use microwave ovens on a limited basis because they

   A. require a large amount of energy.
   B. are difficult to keep clean.
   C. have a low capacity.
   D. require extensive training.

   L.O. 10.2

7. This piece of equipment is simply a large bain marie.

   A. Hot-food holding table
   B. Convection oven
   C. Infrared oven
   D. Low-temperature oven

   L.O. 10.2

8. Which of the following should be placed closest to the receiving dock?

   A. Dishwasher
   B. Ice machine
   C. Walk-in refrigerator
   D. Rangetop stove

   L.O. 10.1

9. Which of the following causes the most havoc if it breaks down during business hours?

   A. Dishwasher
   B. Ice machine
   C. Walk-in refrigerator
   D. Rangetop stove

L.O. 10.2

10. The goal of a public health inspector is to prove to the public that a new restaurant is

    A. affordable.
    B. safe.
    C. fair to its employees.
    D. profitable.

L.O. 10.2

CHAPTER 11

RESTAURANT OPERATIONS AND CONTROL

Learning Objectives

After reading this chapter, students should be able to:

11.1   Describe back-of-the-house operations.

11.2   Describe front-of-the-house operations.

11.3   Identify ways to control food, beverage, and labor costs.

11.4   Discuss methods of guest check control.

Chapter 11 Study Outline

1. In restaurants, the back of the house includes purchasing, receiving, storing, issuing, food preparation, service, sanitation, and administration.

2. The employees who have direct contact with guests are the hosts, bartenders, servers, bussers, and managers, collectively known as the front of the house.

3. Managers forecast a daily guest count by examining historical data, the weather, day of the week, and other factors.

4. The elements of management include planning, organizing, communicating, decision-making, motivation, and control.

5. Calculating the restaurant's food cost percentage on a monthly basis helps a manager control expenses.

6. The formula for calculating food cost percentages is cost divided by sales multiplied by one hundred.

7. Liquor offers the greatest opportunity for abuse or theft. The beverage-storage area should remain locked at all times with only one key available to the manager.

8. In restaurants, the largest variable cost is labor.

    *   On average, front of the house labor costs as a percentage of sales runs just over nine percent

    *   For the back of the house, labor cost as a percentage of sales is approximately thirteen percent.

9. Seat-turnover rates are used to indicate sales volume and to determine the efficiency of the entire operation.

10. Guest checks can be abused but managers can control theft by establishing and enforcing "no ticket-no food" policies.

Chapter 11 Exercises

1. List four stations that are part of a restaurant's back of the house.

    - _____
    - _____
    - _____
    - _____

L.O. 11.1

2. Who is directly responsible for checking that all menu items are prepared in accordance with standardized recipes?

    _____

L.O. 11.1

3. Briefly explain what managers can do to make sure guests receive a favorable first impression of the restaurant.

    _____

    _____

    _____

    _____

L.O. 11.2

4. The Homeland Café buys 6-ounce rib eye steaks for $3.50 each. They are listed on the menu for $15.95. What is the restaurant's food cost percentage?

    _____

L.O. 11.3

5. While taking inventory, the manager of the Homeland Café decided to start by checking the sale of rib eye steaks. The last time he took inventory, there were only 2 steaks left, so he ordered 24 additional steaks. Employees are not allowed to order the steaks for their meals, and there were no reports of spoilage. He now has 4 steaks left in the walk-in. According to the guest check receipts, food revenue from the sale of rib eye steaks is $239.25. What is the current food cost percentage? Does he have a problem?

_____

_____

_____

L.O. 11.3

6. When should new bottles of alcohol be issued from the storage locker?

_____

_____

L.O. 11.3

7. Briefly explain why guest checks need to be controlled by the restaurant's management.

_____

_____

_____

L.O. 11.4

Chapter 11 Check-in

1. Who is usually responsible for the nightly inventory and production sheets for the next day?

   A. Bartender
   B. Prep cook
   C. Chef
   D. Hostess

   L.O. 11.1

2. Managers forecast daily guest counts to anticipate sales and

   A. daily profit margins.
   B. plan lunch specials.
   C. set staffing levels.
   D. set reorder points for perishable items.

   L.O. 11.2

3. The person ultimately responsible for the smooth running of the front of the house is the

   A. server.
   B. bartender.
   C. chef.
   D. manager.

L.O. 11.1

4. To control costs, a restaurant's food cost percentage should be calculated

   A. daily.
   B. weekly.
   C. monthly.
   D. annually.

L.O. 11.3

5. If a domestic beef costs $.75, and the manager establishes a pouring cost of 25%, the beef should sell for

   A. $2.40.
   B. $3.00
   C. $3.40.
   D. $3.75.

L.O. 11.3

6. Which of the following employees should be issued a key to the liquor storage area?

   A. Manager
   B. Chef
   C. Bartender
   D. Hostess

L.O. 11.3

7. The largest variable cost in most restaurants is

   A. equipment leases.
   B. labor.
   C. rent.
   D. property taxes.

L.O. 11.3

8. In a restaurant with 34 tables, what is the minimum number of servers that should be on the floor if they are to handle at least 4 tables each?

   A. 6
   B. 8
   C. 10
   D. 12

L.O. 11.3

9. Seat turnover rates indicate both the volume of sales and the operation's

   A. profitability.
   B. guest-check average.
   C. efficiency.
   D. gross sales.

L.O. 11.4

10. Restaurants use a duplicate-check system as a way to

   A. have records for an IRS audit.
   B. maintain tight control of food sales.
   C. allow servers to place orders in the bar and the kitchen simultaneously.
   D. have a copy if the original is lost.

L.O. 11.4

CHAPTER 12

ORGANIZATION, RECRUITING, AND STAFFING

Learning Objectives

After reading this chapter, students should be able to:

12.1   Describe the processes for creating job and task analyses.

12.2   Describe the components of a job description, and list guidelines for creating one.

12.3   Identify legal issues surrounding hiring and employment.

12.4   Determine the legality of potential interview questions.

Chapter 12 Study Outline

1. Before a foodservice operator can staff his or her operation, it is important to conduct a job analysis to determine which tasks will need to be performed. The two main approaches to job analysis are:

    *   Bottom up, when the jobs already exist but still need to be defined

    *   Top down, when opening a new restaurant

2. The tasks and responsibilities developed through job analysis are written as job descriptions for each position.

3. A job specification lists specific qualifications a person must have to perform tasks listed in the job description.

4. Tasks in each job description can be broken down into exact steps taken to complete the job. This information helps develop a system for training new employees, as well as a guide to evaluate the performance of each individual holding that position.

5. After each position is defined, an organization chart is created to show relationships among various jobs.

6. Several federal laws, including the Civil Rights Act, the Immigration Reform and Control Act (IRCA), and the Americans with Disabilities Act (ADA), regulate what employers may ask and require of employees.

7. Civil rights laws state that employers may not discriminate in employment on the basis of an individual's race, religion, color, sex, national origin, marital status, age, family relationship, mental or physical handicaps, or juvenile record, if it has been cleared.

8. Equal employment opportunity is the legal right of all individuals to be considered for employment and promotion on the basis of their ability and merit.

9. The Equal Employment Opportunity Commission (EEOC) enforces laws requiring equal employment opportunity.

10. The Americans with Disabilities Act (ADA) provides civil-rights protection for people with disabilities. The ADA defines a person with a disability to be an individual who falls within three categories:

    - Someone with a physical or mental impairment that substantially limits one or more major life activities
    - Someone with a history of such an impairment
    - Someone who is perceived as having a disability

11. The ADA affects most employers, and all areas in a restaurant used by the public. By carefully matching jobs with the applicants' abilities, many restaurant owners now employ people who are physically or mentally challenged.

12. AIDS cannot be transmitted through daily routines in a restaurant and is not a valid reason to refuse someone employment.

13. Recruitment, selection, and interviewing are the processes by which prospective employees are screened.

14. The interview process can be daunting for both the applicant and the employer. The interviewer must plan ahead to make sure the setting will put the applicant at ease.

15. When making a hiring decision, remember that attitude is more important than ability.

16. Employment of minors is quite common in the foodservice industry. Some federal regulations control the kind of work minors (ages sixteen and younger) can perform.

17. The Immigration and Control Act of 1986 makes it illegal for employers to employ undocumented aliens.

18. Civil-rights laws forbid discriminatory use of information in selecting employees. Text pages 332–336 list questions that should *not* appear on an application form or mentioned during an interview, as well as good questions that should be asked.

19. The three main hiring objectives in a restaurant are:

    - Hiring people who project the appropriate image for the restaurant
    - Hiring team players
    - Hiring people whose personal and financial requirements can be met by the job

20. Careful selection of employees includes:

    - Checking references
    - Employment testing, where it is valid and reliable
    - Screening out substance abusers

Chapter 12 Exercises

1. List five tasks that should be included in a job description for a server.

   - _____
   - _____
   - _____
   - _____
   - _____

L.O. 12.1

2. What is the difference between a job description and a job specification?

   _____

   _____

   _____

L.O. 12.2

3. What is a job instruction sheet, and who uses it?

   _____

   _____

   _____

L.O. 12.2

4. How has the Americans with Disabilities Act (ADA) affected the restaurant industry?

   _____

   _____

   _____

L.O. 12.3

5. List three areas in a restaurant where minors under the age of sixteen cannot work.

- _____

- _____

- _____

L.O. 12.3

6. Name three documents that can be used to determine the legal status of a prospective employee planning to work in the U.S.

- _____

- _____

- _____

L.O. 12.3

7. Briefly discuss the importance of careful screening of prospective employees prior to the offer of employment.

_____

_____

_____

L.O. 12.3

8. Indicate whether each of the following interview questions is legal (L) or illegal (I). Note that each letter will be used more than once.

_____(1) Are you married?

_____(2) Are you old enough to work here?

_____(3) Where were you born?

_____(4) What year did you graduate from high school?

_____(5) How long were you at your last job?

_____(6) How many hours a week do you want to work?

_____(7) What church do you attend?

_____(8) Who should I contact in case of an emergency?

_____(9) What was the most enjoyable part of your last job?

_____(10) Were you let go from your last job?

L.O. 12.4

Chapter 12 Check-in

1. This examines the tasks and jobs to be performed in a restaurant.

   A. Job analysis
   B. Job description
   C. Job specification
   D. Job-instruction sheet

   L.O. 12.1

2. When developing job analyses for a new restaurant, it is best to use a(n)

   A. bottom-up method.
   B. top-down method.
   C. organizational chart.
   D. manual from a national chain.

   L.O. 12.1

3. This explains the education and skills needed to perform a job.

   A. Job analysis
   B. Job description
   C. Job specification
   D. Job-instruction sheet

   L.O. 12.2

4. Trainers use this list to teach new hires their job.

   A. Job analysis
   B. Job description
   C. Job specification
   D. Job instruction sheet

   L.O. 12.2

5. If an employee believes he/she has been subject to discrimination, a report is filed with the

   A. U.S. Department of Labor.
   B. FDA.
   C. EEOC.
   D. state ABC.

   L.O. 12.3

6. The Americans with Disabilities Act affects

   A. only newly constructed restaurants.
   B. any restaurant that hires disabled employees.
   C. all restaurants, unless they have a drive-through window.
   D. all areas of a restaurant.

   L.O. 123.

7. Which personality trait is best suited for a front-of-house job?

   A. Surly
   B. Shy
   C. Outgoing
   D. Cautious

   L.O. 12.4

8. Employees who are minors are not allowed to

   A. work in freezers.
   B. wrap meat and produce.
   C. work at serving counters.
   D. wash any windows.

   L.O. 12.3

9. Managers should look for new employees

    A. on the Internet.
    B. through referrals from existing employees.
    C. at local career fairs.
    D. All of the above

L.O. 12.4

10. Which of the following questions cannot be asked during an interview?

    A. What are your hobbies and interests?
    B. How would your previous employer describe your work?
    C. Where were you born?
    D. Do you speak more than one language?

L.O. 12.4

CHAPTER 13

EMPLOYEE TRAINING AND DEVELOPMENT

Learning Objectives

After reading this chapter, students should be able to:

13.1   List the goals of an orientation program.

13.2   Compare and contrast behavior modeling and learner-controlled instruction.

13.3   List guidelines for effective trainers.

13.4   Describe characteristics of effective managers.

13.5   Describe elements of an effective training program.

Chapter 13 Study Outline

1. As it becomes more difficult to compete with other businesses for qualified and competent employees, foodservice managers must invest more resources—both time and money—in hiring, training, developing, and retaining the best people.

2. A good training program begins with a systematic new-employee orientation meant to introduce new employees to the culture, environment, and shared values of the company. The orientation period is a chance for the operation to give a positive impression to new employees so they will give their new jobs their best efforts.

3. Training is no longer defined as simply telling a new employee to follow a more experienced employee around for a day or two before getting started. The most successful operations have well-planned, thorough, and ongoing training programs for all employees.

4. The overall goal of training is to instill and develop the proper attitude and job skills that customers expect from the restaurant's employees.

5. Employee development gives employees the ability to come up with flexible solutions to problem situations.

6. For training to be effective, the trainer must be well acquainted with, although not necessarily proficient in, the tasks being taught.

7. The more tasks and jobs are broken down into separate steps, the more likely employees are to learn them.

8. Trainees must be given a chance to practice everything they are taught before having to perform these new concepts and skills on the job.

9. Learner-Controlled Instruction (LCI) is a training system in which employees are responsible for learning new tasks and information at their own pace, and for completing tasks as a result. This can save management time and training costs.

10. Liquor liability is an area in which employee training is especially important. Dram shop laws make managers and employees responsible for accidents caused by customers who drive away from the operation while intoxicated.

11. Managers must also be effective leaders, encouraging and motivating employees to move the organization forward.

12. Leaders see problems as challenges, and provide opportunities for their employees to overcome obstacles. However, if the same problems persist, employees will become frustrated.

Chapter 13 Exercises

1. List three of the goals of an orientation program.

    * _____

    * _____

    * _____

L.O. 13.1

2. Why is it more efficient to train a new employee systematically, rather than by observation?

    _____

    _____

    _____

L.O. 13.5

3. What is the importance of emphasizing employee development?

    _____

    _____

    _____

L.O. 13.5

4. What are the benefits of Learner-Controlled Instruction?

_____

_____

_____

L.O. 13.5

5. Briefly explain why the manager of a restaurant is similar to a football coach.

_____

_____

_____

L.O. 13.4

6. Why is communication with employees so important for a manager's success?

_____

_____

_____

L.O. 13.4

7. How should a manager react to each of the following situations?

   a. A server rushing through the kitchen collides with a prep cook, knocking a large bowl of prepared food to the floor.

   _____

   _____

   _____

   b. An exceptionally boisterous crowd has just left the restaurant, and their server has worked very hard to keep them happy.

   _____

   _____

   _____

c. The wrong person accepted delivery of a crate of produce.

_____

_____

_____

L.O. 13.4

Chapter 13 Check-in

1. The main goal of an orientation program is to
   A. determine the job skills of a new employee.
   B. explain why this restaurant is better than the competition.
   C. establish a bond between the new employee and the restaurant.
   D. introduce the new employee to regular customers.

L.O. 13.1

2. Trainees will learn a new job more quickly if the job instructions are
   A. brief.
   B. listed on a big poster.
   C. available on the Internet for home study.
   D. delivered in an authoritative tone of voice.

L.O. 13.5

3. The best trainers use this trait to improve the learning process.
   A. Critical attention to detail
   B. Enthusiasm
   C. Cynical humor
   D. Silent observation

L.O. 13.5

4. The best way to train new employees is by having them
   A. watch corporate videos.
   B. use a hands-on method.
   C. take written tests.
   D. watch other employees in action.

L.O. 13.4

5. When an employee has made an error, the manager should
   A. use it as an opportunity to teach the entire staff a lesson.
   B. let it go if it is not too important.
   C. tell the trainer to take care of it.
   D. use a praise-criticize-praise technique.

L.O. 13.4

6. The volume of part-time employees in restaurants can be a problem because
   A. it is difficult to find enough employees.
   B. the training process must include a large group of people.
   C. training can take place only when the restaurant is busy.
   D. it requires additional training for employees who are less motivated.

L.O. 13.5

7. Employees who are given job standards to achieve on their own rate are taught through

    A. step-by-step instruction.
    B. behavior modification.
    C. learner-controlled instruction.
    D. assertiveness training.

L.O. 13.5

8. Effective managers see problems as a

    A. way to teach employees new lessons.
    B. challenge.
    C. personal affront.
    D. frustrating experience.

L.O. 13.4

9. Managers must remember that the best motivational tool at their disposal is

    A. discipline.
    B. praise.
    C. the right to fire for cause.
    D. sales competitions.

L.O. 13.4

10. Employees will be more motivated in their jobs if managers

    A. hand out job-instruction sheets on a daily basis.
    B. post employee-development guidelines in the break room.
    C. explain what they believe is important.
    D. socialize with employees after work hours.

L.O. 13.4

CHAPTER 14

SERVICE AND CUSTOMER RELATIONS

Learning Objectives

After reading this chapter, you should be able to:

14.1   Describe characteristics of effective servers and greeters.

14.2   Identify the seven commandments of customer service.

14.3   List guidelines for handling customer complaints.

Chapter 14 Study Outline

1. The most common reason customers give for not returning to a foodservice operation has nothing to do with food or prices or the competition—it is poor or indifferent service.

2. Servers have enormous influence on the impressions guests have of an operation.

3. In a competitive environment, servers begin to look at the customer as an opponent. It can devolve into a game of one-upsmanship among the servers, destroying a customer's enjoyment of the restaurant.

4. A customer's first impression comes from the host or hostess at the front desk, whose main job is to welcome guests and facilitate seating arrangements.

5. The best server is both a performer and a salesperson, attending to each detail and manipulating events in such a way that the guest is left with a positive experience.

6. The formality or informality of employees must be appropriate for the particular operation's customers, theme, décor, and mission.

7. Servers can greatly influence the operation's profits—and their own tips—by "selling" the menu and its items. It is every manager's responsibility to train servers to give the best possible service, so customers will not only come back, but also tell their friends about the operation.

8. When employees hear complaints from customers, they should listen carefully to everything the customer says and act promptly to correct the situation.

9. Belligerent customers can be asked to leave, or the police can be called.

Chapter 14 Exercises

1. Customers rank _____ as the primary reason for choosing a restaurant.
L.O. 14.1

2. Restaurant patrons complain the most about a restaurant's _____ _____.
L.O. 14.1

3. Servers often see themselves as _____, with two shows a day.
L.O. 14.1

4. A person entering a restaurant to dine alone often feels like an _____.
L.O. 14.1

5. When servers compete to see who makes the most tips, service quality usually suffers

because the _____ is seen as an opponent.

L.O. 14.1

6. The _____ is the employee who sets the tone for guests' entire

dining experience.

L.O. 14.1

7. When it comes to customer service, the first and most important commandment is to

always _____ _____ _____.

L.O. 14.2

8. According to the "Seven Commandments of Customer Service," why is it acceptable to
sometimes bend the rules?

_____

_____

_____

L.O. 14.2

9. When dealing with a difficult customer, explain why it is important to:

a. be diplomatic.

_____

_____

b. remain calm.

_____

_____

c. listen carefully.

_____

_____

d. empathize.

_____

_____

e. control your voice.

_____

_____

f. obtain all the facts.

_____

_____

g. respond immediately.

_____

_____

L.O. 14.2

Chapter 14 Check-in

1. Servers often have the most problems from guests seated

   A. in a booth.
   B. in open spaces.
   C. alone by the back wall.
   D. near the kitchen.

   L.O. 14.1

2. The main job of a host or hostess is to

   A. improve liquor receipts by sending all guests to the bar immediately.
   B. represent the restaurant and facilitate guest seating.
   C. call out names of patrons when seats are available.
   D. assist bussers to clear tables quickly.

   L.O. 14.1

3. Servers often make more money in tips than in salary, and sometimes see themselves as

   A. team players.
   B. management.
   C. independent businesspeople.
   D. contractors.

   L.O. 14.1

4. A hard-sell technique is best for patrons who are

   A. celebrating.
   B. eating alone.
   C. regular customers.
   D. traveling.

   L.O. 14.1

5. When customers have a problem, they most often

   A. confront the nearest server in a loud voice.
   B. write a letter to the manager after leaving.
   C. do not mention it.
   D. call the local Better Business Bureau.

   L.O. 14.3

6. If it is busy and something goes wrong, a server should never

   A. make excuses.
   B. correct it unless the customer complains.
   C. alert the manager.
   D. enlist the help of other servers.

   L.O. 14.3

7. When a guest orders incorrectly, the server should

   A. make sure the guest knows it is not the server's fault.
   B. convince the guest that what was ordered is the better meal.
   C. call over the manager to get his opinion.
   D. accept the responsibility and correct the problem.

   L.O. 14.3

8. If a disgruntled customer is yelling, the manager should
   A. speak loud enough to be heard by the customer.
   B. ask the customer to step outside to discuss the situation.
   C. speak calmly and diffuse the situation.
   D. call the police.

   L.O. 14.3

9. When listening to complaints, it is best to
   A. nod your head and roll your eyes.
   B. doodle on the guest check.
   C. try a casual touch on the guest's shoulder.
   D. empathize.

   L.O. 14.3

10. To prevent altercations, restaurants that cater to teenagers should
    A. establish and enforce clear ground rules.
    B. reduce the lights to encourage an intimate dining experience.
    C. pull condiments off the dining floor after school hours.
    D. hire a school teacher as night manager.

    L.O. 14. 3

CHAPTER 15

RESTAURANT TECHNOLOGY

Learning Objectives

After reading this chapter, you should be able to:

15.1   Identify the main types of restaurant industry technologies.

15.2   List and describe the main types of software programs.

15.3   Identify factors to consider when choosing technology for a restaurant.

Chapter 15 Study Outline

1. Restaurant technology is divided into two parts, front- and back-of-house systems that are sometimes integrated.

2. Product management software tracks products through each stage of the inventory cycle and can automatically reorder items as needed.

3. Handheld bar-code readers can speed up inventory and calculate food cost percentages more accurately.

4. Menu-management programs evaluate purchasing, and compare actual food usage to expected food usage.

5. Labor-management systems handle both front- and back-of-house employees for scheduling, recruitment, and other human-resource issues.

6. Daily financial reports and balance sheet allow managers to make more informed decisions.

7. Larger chains are using the Internet to train employees, using computerized programs rather than printed and cumbersome manuals.

8. In the front of the house, there are several point-of-sale systems available:

    •   NCR's Human Factors Engineering evaluates store performance and identifies areas for improvement.

    •   Aloha's POS communicates between the kitchen and waitstaff, sending orders to different stations of the kitchen, notifying servers when items run out, and measuring the performance of each server. It can also process credit card transactions and collect vital customer information.

- ASI's Write-on Handheld POS system lets servers write out orders and send them directly to the kitchen. The entire menu is loaded in the unit, helping with sales, corresponding orders to guests, and telling servers when the kitchen runs out of an item.

9. POS systems are growing more and more sophisticated, integrating sales with inventory, labor costs, and financial reporting.

10. Guests can visit a restaurant's Web site to review the menu, obtain driving directions, check parking availability, reserve a table, and interact with management.

11. Coffee houses are installing high-speed Internet access as a way to attract additional guests.

Chapter 15 Exercises

1. Briefly explain how product-management software helps managers control inventory.

_____

_____

_____

L.O. 15.1

2. Which software system is used to determine which coupon programs are working the best?

_____

L.O. 15.1

3. List two ways in which labor-management systems help managers control expenses.

- _____

- _____

L.O. 15.1

4. List three reasons why some POS systems fail to improve productivity and customer service.

- _____

- _____

- _____

L.O. 15.3

5. Which group works with restaurant managers to improve performance and increase profits by examining existing software systems?

_____

L.O, 15.3

6. What is the benefit of Aloha's Kitchen Display System?

_____

_____

L.O. 15.3

7. In addition to taking orders, list three other features offered by the Write-On Handheld POS system.

- _____

- _____

- _____

L.O. 15.3

8. Briefly discuss why a dinner house should invest in building a Web site.

_____

_____

_____

L.O. 15.3

Chapter 15 Check-in

1. Which software system reorders inventory items when they fall below par-stock levels?

   A. MenuLink
   B. ASI WriteOn
   C. Aloha Customer Management
   D. Chef Tec

   L.O. 15.1

2. Laser bar-code readers are used to

   A. manage table-turnover rates.
   B. speed up inventory reporting.
   C. inform servers when specials run out.
   D. track employees on the floor.

   L.O. 15.1

3. This system helps managers better control their biggest controllable expense.

   A. TimePro
   B. Aloha's Table Service
   C. ASI's Write-On
   D. Maitre'D POS

   L.O. 15.2

4. Instead of printed manuals, large chain restaurants are using

   A. POS handhelds.
   B. e-learning systems.
   C. NCR's HFE teams.
   D. Aloha's Kitchen Display System

   L.O. 15.2

5. If a new POS system does not increase productivity, managers can enlist the skills of

   A. TimePro.
   B. e-learning systems.
   C. NCR's HFE teams.
   D. Aloha's Kitchen Display System.

   L.O. 15.2

6. This system routes orders to different back-of-house workstations.

   A. TimePro.
   B. e-learning systems.
   C. NCR's HFE teams.
   D. Aloha's Kitchen Display System.

   L.O. 15.2

7. Which Aloha system tracks vital customer information?

   A. Table Service
   B. Customer Management
   C. Kitchen Display System
   D. Event Scheduler

   L.O. 15.2

8. ASI's Write-On Handheld speeds up table-turnover rates because

   A. customers can fill out their own orders.
   B. it routes orders to the right kitchen station.
   C. guests never receive the wrong order.
   D. servers do not have to enter orders twice.

   L.O. 15.2

9. Restaurants are building Web sites to

   A. take reservations.
   B. preview special events.
   C. provide driving and parking instructions.
   D. All of the above

   L.O. 15.1

10. To increase guest services, some coffee houses are installing

   A. high-speed Internet access.
   B. wireless pagers.
   C. handheld ordering devices.
   D. e-learning software.

   L.O. 15.1

Practice Test

1. Restaurant owners believe that their success ultimately depends on

   A. the location of the restaurant.
   B. extensive advertising and promotions.
   C. hard work and excellent people skills.
   D. the design of the kitchen and dining room.

   L.O. 1.1

2. One of the biggest liabilities of restaurant ownership is

   A. intense competition.
   B. finding affordable fresh produce.
   C. serving the public.
   D. health risks caused by long hours.

   L.O. 1.2

3. This popular early-American tavern drink was made with rum, beer, eggs, and spices.

   A. Flip
   B. Wassail
   C. Patriot punch
   D. Caribbean cocktail

   L.O. 1.3

4. Family-owned restaurants have a higher success rate because

   A. banks prefer to lend to family businesses.
   B. the cost of employing family members is lower.
   C. their children can eat for free.
   D. all their friends prefer to eat there.

   L.O. 1.4

5. The least expensive way to open your own restaurant is to

   A. build a new building.
   B. purchase a franchise.
   C. buy an existing restaurant and update its image.
   D. accept a management position with a large chain restaurant.

   L.O. 1.4

6. The best way for a person to find out if the restaurant industry is the right career choice is to

   A. watch a lot of cooking shows.
   B. attend the National Restaurant Association trade show.
   C. read as many restaurant magazines as possible.
   D. work in a restaurant similar to the type he/she wants to own.

   L.O. 1.4

7. The goal of a quick-service operation is to

   A. serve the maximum number of customers in the least amount of time.
   B. help customers relax and enjoy the dining experience.
   C. develop menu items that reflect the restaurant's ethnic roots.
   D. encourage employees to invest in their skills and become franchise owners.

   L.O. 2.1

8. Which quick-service chain developed Braille overlays on its cash register keys?

   A. KFC
   B. Carl's Jr.
   C. Burger King
   D. Wendy's

   L.O. 2.3

9. This type of restaurant relies more heavily on selling merchandise than on food quality.

   A. Fine-dining operations
   B. Ethnic restaurants
   C. Theme restaurants
   D. Steakhouses

   L.O. 2.1

10. During its early years, this restaurant opened additional stores to appear successful but did not become profitable until it had five locations.

    A. KFC
    B. Wendy's
    C. Subway
    D. Delmonico's

    L.O. 2.3

11. In the U.S., Cantonese food is best known for its

    A. dim sum filled with meat or seafood.
    B. use of hot peppers.
    C. use of cilantro and coconut milk.
    D. blend of hot and sour flavors.

    L.O. 2.1

12. To increase home-delivery sales in affluent neighborhoods, some operations

    A. deliver only to the service entrance.
    B. prepare meals in attractive baskets.
    C. make drivers wear tuxedos.
    D. partner with Meals on Wheels.

    L.O. 2.1

13. These restaurant operators often hire publicists to promote their talents.

    A. Chef-owners
    B. Theme-restaurant owners
    C. Franchise owners
    D. Small-franchise owners

    L.O. 2.2

14. A restaurant's concept can be strengthened if the name chosen

    A. is a pun.
    B. sounds similar to the name of an established restaurant.
    C. establishes its identity.
    D. reminds people of a recent hit movie.

    L.O. 3.1

15. To determine the viability of a new restaurant concept, it is best to

    A. hire a marketing firm to conduct a telephone survey.
    B. assess the number of people in the target market and determine their demographic profile.
    C. ask patrons at other restaurants in the area if they might be interested in the concept.
    D. discuss your ideas with friends who live in the area.

    L.O. 3.2

16. One of the main reasons why successful restaurants eventually fail is due to

    A. fire.
    B. employee theft.
    C. negative changes in the market's demographics.
    D. poorly executed sales promotions.

L.O. 3.2

17. Which type of restaurant generally offers the most space per guest?

    A. Family restaurant
    B. Coffee shop
    C. Quick-service operation
    D. Luxury restaurant

L.O. 3.6

18. Which of the following information should not be included in a mission statement?

    A. Purpose of the enterprise
    B. Anticipated profit margin
    C. Strategy of the business
    D. Expected behavioral and ethical standards of employees

L.O. 3.6

19. Which type of restaurant is most concerned with its visibility and accessibility from a major highway?

    A. Family restaurant
    B. Fine-dining restaurant
    C. Quick-serve chain restaurant
    D. Ethnic restaurant

L.O. 3.5

20. When choosing a new location, chain restaurants look for

    A. traffic generators.
    B. zoning moratoriums.
    C. low-density housing tracts.
    D. busy streets.

L.O. 3.5

21. Knockout criteria is used to

    A. determine the possibility of expanding an existing building.
    B. completely destroy the competition.
    C. eliminate a site from consideration.
    D. win zoning board approval for a controversial site.

L.O. 3.7

22. In the dining room, the design element that is most important is

    A. window treatments.
    B. lighting.
    C. table linens and place settings.
    D. employee uniforms.

L.O. 3.6

23. A well-defined business plan not only helps a restaurant succeed, but also can be used to

    A. obtain financing.
    B. eliminate competition.
    C. develop employee training manuals.
    D. streamline purchasing.

L.O. 4.1

24. A market assessment analyzes

    A. local property taxes.
    B. the number of investors interested
       in the new restaurant.
    C. the community, the customers,
       and the competition.
    D. the benefits the restaurant offers
       its customers.

    L.O. 4.3

25. Which of the following is an example
    of contribution pricing?

    A. Changing an item's calculated
       price from $7.80 to $7.95 to
       appear more attractive
    B. Reducing an item's price to
       compete with another restaurant's
       pricing
    C. Drastically reducing the
       calculated price of an item to an
       acceptable amount
    D. Increasing the price to improve its
       profit margin

    L.O. 4.4

26. *Sales promotion* is best described as

    A. materials meant to remind servers
       to upsell certain items.
    B. efforts to communicate with the
       media and community.
    C. paid communications to the
       public.
    D. activities meant to persuade
       customers to visit the restaurant.

    L.O. 4.4

27. When forecasting sales, managers
    estimate the average guest check and

    A. labor costs.
    B. guest counts.
    C. lease payments.
    D. food costs.

    L.O. 5.1

28. Which of the following is
    a variable cost?

    A. Real estate taxes
    B. Depreciation on equipment
    C. Food sales
    D. Insurance premiums

    L.O. 5.3

29. The Small Business Administration

    A. lends money for new home
       mortgages to small business
       owners.
    B. guarantees loans to small
       businesses.
    C. finds banks willing to lend to
       small businesses.
    D. teaches small-business owners
       how to run their operations.

    L.O. 5.4

30. The selling price of a restaurant is
    determined by its real estate value and
    its value as a

    A. tourist destination.
    B. job creator for the local economy.
    C. profit generator.
    D. traffic generator.

    L.O. 5.6

31. Which type of business organization is the least complicated?

    A. Partnership
    B. Sole proprietorship
    C. Corporation
    D. S corporation

    L.O. 6.1

32. In this type of business entity, all of the restaurant's debts are the responsibility of the owner.

    A. Partnership
    B. Sole proprietorship
    C. Corporation
    D. S corporation

    L.O. 6.2

33. Which federal agency oversees anti-discrimination laws?

    A. National Labor Relations Board
    B. FDA
    C. EEOC
    D. FCC

    L.O. 6.3

34. To make sure a menu item is prepared with the same quality and quantity every time, restaurant owners rely on

    A. signature items.
    B. menu analysis.
    C. standardized recipes.
    D. product specifications.

    L.O. 7.1

35. Many restaurants are offering low-fat menu items

    A. to satisfy the demands of health-conscious customers.
    B. to reduce food costs.
    C. because the pans are easier to clean.
    D. because today's chefs prefer to cook on non-stick skillets.

    L.O. 7.1

36. School cafeterias typically use which type of menu?

    A. À la carte
    B. Seasonal
    C. Cyclical
    D. Degustation

    L.O. 7.2

37. The design and layout of a menu should always

    A. include pictures of signature items.
    B. complement the style and décor of the restaurant.
    C. leave space for daily specials.
    D. contain icons pointing out employee favorites.

    L.O. 7.4

38. Before a restaurant owner can sell beer or wine, he or she must obtain a license from the

    A. FDA.
    B. Department of Alcoholic Beverage Control.
    C. Department of Agriculture.
    D. DEA.

    L.O. 8.1

39. For sanitary reasons, bar glassware should be washed in a sink with

    A. a rubber mat at the bottom.
    B. a spray attachment.
    C. three compartments.
    D. a bleach dispenser.

L.O. 8.2

40. An entrée that is cooked in red wine should be served with

    A. wine of the same variety.
    B. white wine.
    C. sparkling wine.
    D. port.

L.O. 8.3

41. The dram shop laws state that

    A. persons under the age of eighteen cannot purchase alcohol.
    B. minors are not allowed to serve alcohol.
    C. applicants for a liquor license must notify the newspapers.
    D. owners are liable for injuries caused by intoxicated customers.

L.O. 8.4

42. To avoid thefts of alcohol, most restaurant managers

    A. are also bartenders.
    B. conduct weekly audits.
    C. buy alcohol only from local wholesalers.
    D. invest in a speed gun.

L.O. 8.5

43. Restaurants use what tool to control the quality of the food they purchase?

    A. Walk-in refrigerators
    B. Menu analysis
    C. Production sheets
    D. Product specifications

L.O. 9.1

44. The amount of time a food product can be stored without a noticeable loss in quality is called its

    A. product specification.
    B. shelf life.
    C. par stock.
    D. reorder point.

L.O. 9.2

45. Restaurant owners should call vendors frequently in order to

    A. establish a friendly relationship.
    B. let them know you are still in business.
    C. stay abreast of changing prices.
    D. compare their customer service.

L.O. 9.3

46. Restaurants typically pay more for food items than a typical shopper because

    A. the supplier delivers and sells on credit.
    B. shoppers can use coupons.
    C. restaurants always receive higher quality fresh produce.
    D. restaurants sometimes offer food that is out of season.

L.O. 9.3

47. In order to make sure no stored food gets too old, restaurants use a

    A. first-in, first-out rotation system.
    B. last-in, first-out rotation system.
    C. first-in, last-out rotation system.
    D. last-in, last-out rotation system.

    L.O. 9.3

48. Which agency judges the quality of meat according to a grading system?

    A. FDA
    B. National Livestock and Meat Board
    C. USDA
    D. EPA

    L.O. 9.4

49. The overall objective of kitchen-layout planning is to

    A. minimize the steps of staff.
    B. maximize storage space.
    C. avoid spills.
    D. encourage team building.

    L.O. 10.1

50. When designing a kitchen's traffic pattern, this should be set off to one side.

    A. Pre-prep area
    B. Dishwasher
    C. Walk-in refrigerator
    D. Dry-storage area

    L.O. 10.1

51. According to the America Gas Association, the most efficient kitchen design is

    A. circular.
    B. square.
    C. rectangular.
    D. oval.

    L.O. 10.1

52. Open kitchens are more expensive to build because

    A. health-department rules require extra space between the kitchen and dining room.
    B. all the kitchen equipment must be new.
    C. it takes highly skilled architects to design them.
    D. they require extra noise-reducing ceiling tiles.

    L.O. 10.1

53. Which type of flooring material should not be used in a kitchen?

    A. Quarry tile
    B. Carpeting
    C. Asphalt tile
    D. Sealed concrete

    L.O. 10.1

54. The type of equipment an operation uses depends primarily on which of the following?

    A. Manager's cooking skills
    B. Average business volume
    C. Cash flow
    D. Menu

    L.O. 10.2

55. The conveyor broiler used by some hamburger quick-service restaurants is an example of kitchen equipment that

    A. eliminates the need for cooking skills.
    B. is multi-functional.
    C. doubles as a centerpiece in an exhibition kitchen.
    D. cooks by circulating hot air.

    L.O. 10.2

56. Grooved griddles are replacing broilers in some restaurants because

   A. they make better cross-hatch marks in meats.
   B. they use less fuel.
   C. they are easier to clean.
   D. they eliminate the need for cooking skills.

L.O. 10.2

57. This type of oven uses a fan to speed up cooking times.

   A. Low-temperature oven
   B. Convection oven
   C. Microwave oven
   D. Conventional oven

L.O. 10.2

58. To keep kitchen equipment from breaking down, managers should

   A. only buy new equipment.
   B. replace existing equipment every five years.
   C. establish a rigorous maintenance schedule.
   D. never buy equipment with moving parts.

L.O. 10.2

59. Which of the following is considered a part of a restaurant's back of the house?

   A. Accounting
   B. Bartending
   C. Hostess station
   D. Coffee station

L.O. 11.1

60. In most restaurants, the person responsible for the smooth running of the back of the house is the

   A. hostess.
   B. dishwasher.
   C. chef.
   D. prep cook.

L.O. 11.1

61. The person ultimately responsible for running the front of the house smoothly is the

   A. hostess.
   B. chef.
   C. manager.
   D. server.

L.O. 11.2

62. Standardized recipes and weighing and measuring food items are examples of

   A. portion control.
   B. product specifications.
   C. menu analysis.
   D. quality standards.

L.O. 11.3

63. These people are often asked to report on the quality of a restaurant's products and services.

   A. Regular customers
   B. Other employees
   C. Investors
   D. Secret shoppers

L.O. 11.3

64. This type of restaurant tends to have a low guest-check average.

    A. Steakhouse
    B. Quick-service restaurant
    C. Luxury dinner house
    D. Theme restaurant

L.O. 11.3

65. One way to control guest checks is to have servers

    A. number their own checks.
    B. supply their own checks.
    C. act as their own cashiers.
    D. conduct audits of their used checks.

L.O. 11.4

66. This is used to select, train, and set performance standards of employees.

    A. Job analysis
    B. Job description
    C. Job specification
    D. Task analysis

L.O. 12.2

67. This is used to explain the lines of communication and relationships between jobs.

    A. Job-instruction sheet
    B. Job description
    C. Organizational chart
    D. Production sheets

L.O. 12.2

68. During an initial interview, an applicant should be

    A. tested for drug abuse.
    B. asked to take phone orders.
    C. required to work one shift without pay to determine his/her interest.
    D. made to feel comfortable.

L.O. 12.3

69. Which federal regulations make it illegal to discriminate against legal immigrants to the U.S.?

    A. Americans with Disabilities Act
    B. Equal Employment Opportunity Commission
    C. Immigrant Reform and Control Act
    D. Department of Labor

L.O. 12.3

70. Which of the following questions can be asked at an interview?

    A. Do you have any relatives currently employed here?
    B. Where were your parents born?
    C. Have you ever applied for workers' compensation?
    D. Have you ever taken a class on food safety?

L.O. 12.4

71. The goal of employee development is to

    A. increase the number of managers at the restaurant.
    B. promote problem-solving skills.
    C. produce robot-like behavior.
    D. correct bad habits among employees.

L.O. 13.1

72. Which of the following is generally true in an operation with a well-designed employee-training program?

    A. Employees leave once their training is over.

    B. Employees who successfully complete the program are promoted to management.

    C. Employees are unclear about how their position fits into the organization as a whole.

    D. Employee turnover is lower.

L.O. 13.1

73. In Learning Controlled Instruction, an employee's training is directed and monitored by the

    A. employee's supervisor.

    B. operation manager.

    C. employee.

    D. head chef.

L.O. 13.2

74. Which of the following behaviors is considered part of effective leadership?

    A. Discussing an employee's mistakes in front of other employees

    B. Sharing operational information with employees

    C. Accepting new ideas only from senior employees

    D. Talking with employees only when there are problems

L.O. 13.4

75. The most common reason why customers do not return to a restaurant is unhappiness with the

    A. quality of the food.

    B. quantity of food served.

    C. quality of the service.

    D. décor.

L.O. 14.1

76. Which of the following is not one of the "Seven Commandments of Customer Service?"

    A. Tell the truth.

    B. Listen actively.

    C. Be a fantastic fixer.

    D. Break the rules.

L.O. 14.2

77. If a guest's dinner must be returned to the kitchen, it is best to

    A. comp the entire table's dinner bill.

    B. take all entrées back, keep them warm, and serve everyone at the same time.

    C. call over the manager to investigate the problem.

    D. explain to the guest why the problem occurred.

L.O. 14.3

78. This software system can import purchases from a vendor's online ordering system.

    A. Chef Tec

    B. TimePro

    C. Sure POS 700

    D. Aloha's Table Service

L.O. 15.2

79. The device that prompts servers to ask about cooking temperatures is
    A. Chef Tec
    B. TimePro
    C. Write-On
    D. NCR's HFE
    L.O. 15.2

80. To reduce the amount of time employees spend on the phone, owners are
    A. installing high-speed Internet access connections.
    B. building Web sites.
    C. installing pay phones.
    D. buying wireless pagers.
    L.O. 15.2

Practice Test Answer Key

1.	C	p. 4	31.	B	p. 163	61. C	p. 290
2.	D	p. 4	32.	B	p. 164	62. A	p. 291
3.	A	p. 6	33.	C	pp. 179–180	63. D	p. 291
4.	B	p. 6	34.	C	p. 189	64. B	p. 307
5.	C	pp. 7–8	35.	A	pp. 193–194	65. C	p. 305
6.	D	p. 13	36.	C	p. 204	66. B	p. 310
7.	A	p. 21	37.	B	p. 209	67. C	p. 317
8.	B	p. 24	38.	B	p. 217	68. D	p. 321
9.	C	p. 39	39.	C	p. 223	69. C	p. 328
10.	C	pp. 28–29	40.	A	p. 230	70. D	pp. 332–336
11.	A	p. 38	41.	D	p. 232	71. B	p. 347
12.	B	p. 47	42.	B	p. 232	72. D	p. 345
13.	A	p. 42	43.	D	p. 246	73. C	p. 354
14.	C	pp. 52–54	44.	B	p. 248	74. B	p. 358
15.	B	pp. 56–57	45.	C	p. 250	75. C	p. 367
16.	C	p. 64	46.	A	p. 250	76. D	pp. 371–372
17.	D	p. 74	47.	A	p. 257	77. B	p. 378
18.	B	pp. 79–80	48.	C	pp. 254–255	78. A	p. 383
19.	C	pp. 80–82	49.	A	p. 262	79. C	p. 393
20.	A	pp. 81–82	50.	B	p. 262	80. B	p. 397
21.	C	p. 84	51.	C	p. 264		
22.	B	p. 93	52.	D	p. 266		
23.	A	p. 99	53.	B	p. 268		
24.	C	p. 105	54.	D	p. 270		
25.	C	p. 113	55.	A	p. 271		
26.	D	p. 115	56.	B	p. 274		
27.	B	p. 129	57.	B	p. 274		
28.	C	p. 133	58.	C	p. 281		
29.	B	p. 145	59.	A	p. 286		
30.	C	p. 158	60.	C	p. 286		

Chapter Check-in Answer Key

Chapter 1

1.	B	p. 3	5.	B	p. 5	9.	B	p. 8
2.	D	p. 4	6.	C	p. 5	10.	B	p. 11
3.	C	p. 13	7.	A	p. 6			
4.	C	p. 4	8.	A	p. 7			

Chapter 2

1.	B	p. 18	5.	B	p. 30	9.	C	p. 45
2.	C	p. 33	6.	D	p. 22	10.	C	p. 44
3.	D	p. 36	7.	D	pp. 41–42			
4.	A	p. 38	8.	B	p. 23			

Chapter 3

1.	C	p. 52	5.	C	p. 67	9.	B	p. 90
2.	D	p. 51	6.	A	p. 79	10.	C	pp. 84-85
3.	B	p. 51	7.	A	pp. 81–82			
4.	A	p. 64	8.	C	p. 82			

Chapter 4

1.	B	p. 99	5.	D	p. 105	9.	B	p. 113
2.	B	p. 102	6.	C	p. 111	10.	A	p. 119
3.	C	p. 103	7.	A	p. 108			
4.	A	pp. 103–104	8.	D	p. 109			

Chapter 5

1.	B	p. 148	5.	C	p. 151	9.	C	p. 155
2.	A	p. 132	6.	B	p. 146	10.	A	p. 155
3.	D	p. 133	7.	D	p. 151			
4.	C	p. 135	8.	C	pp. 147–148			

Chapter 6

1.	A	p. 163	5.	C	p. 172	9.	C	p. 179
2.	C	p. 166	6.	A	p. 181	10.	B	p. 184
3.	A	p. 164	7.	B	p. 173			
4.	C	p. 172	8.	C	p. 175			

Chapter 7

1.	C	p. 188	5.	C	p. 195	9.	A	p. 208
2.	D	p. 189	6.	A	p. 200	10.	C	p. 213
3.	B	p. 190	7.	D	p. 205			
4.	B	p. 194	8.	C	p. 204			

Chapter 8

1.	C	p. 217	5.	A	p. 224	9.	D	p. 231
2.	D	p. 219	6.	C	p. 229	10.	C	p. 232
3.	B	pp. 220–221	7.	B	p. 226			
4.	A	p. 222	8.	B	p. 231			

Chapter 9

1.	D	p. 246	5.	B	p. 253	9.	C	p. 258
2.	B	p. 249	6.	A	pp. 254–255	10.	C	p. 258
3.	B	p. 248	7.	A	p. 255			
4.	C	p. 250	8.	D	pp. 257–258			

Chapter 10

1.	B	p. 265	5.	B	p. 274	9.	A	p. 281
2.	D	p. 268	6.	C	p. 275	10.	B	p. 282
3.	A	p. 272	7.	A	p. 277			
4.	B	p. 273	8.	C	p. 278			

Chapter 11

1.	C	p. 286	5.	B	p. 291	9.	C	p. 307
2.	C	p. 287	6.	A	p. 296	10.	B	pp. 305–306
3.	D	p. 290	7.	B	p. 298			
4.	C	p. 291	8.	B	p. 300			

Chapter 12

1.	A	p. 310	5.	C	p. 328	9.	D	p. 319
2.	B	p. 310	6.	D	p. 330	10.	C	p. 333
3.	C	p. 310	7.	C	p. 322			
4.	D	p. 316	8.	A	p. 326			

Chapter 13

1.	C							
2.		p. 343	6.	D	p. 347	10.	B	p. 359
3.	A	p. 344	7.	D	p. 346	11.	C	p. 359
4.	B	pp. 345–346	8.	C	p. 354			
5.	B	p. 343	9.	B	p. 357			

Chapter 14

1. B p. 366	5. C p. 372	9. D p. 377
2. B p. 368	6. A p. 372	10. A p. 378
3. C p. 369	7. D p. 375	
4. A p. 370	8. C p. 376	

Chapter 15

1. D p. 383	5. C p. 389	9. D p. 397
2. B p. 384	6. D p. 391	10. A p. 397
3. A p. 388	7. B p. 391	
4. B p. 389	8. D p. 393